The EveryWoman's Guide to Marathoning

The EveryWoman's Guide to Marathoning:
Inspiration and Training for Beginners to Advanced Runners

Wendy Robbins and Alyce Vilines

PENDRAGON PUBLISHING
CHICAGO

The EveryWoman's Guide to Marathoning:
Inspiration and Training for Beginners to Advanced Runners
Copyright© 2006 Wendy Robbins & Alyce Vilines

ISBN 10 1-932965-05-X (trade paper)
ISBN 13 978-1932965-05-6 (trade paper)

Library of Congress Cataloging-in-Publication Data:
Robbins, Wendy, 1960-
    The everywoman's guide to marathoning : inspiration and training
for beginners to advance runners / Wendy Robbins and Alyce Vilines.
      p. cm.
    Includes index.
    ISBN-13: 978-1-932965-05-6 (pbk.)
    ISBN-10: 1-932965-05-X (pbk.)
    1. Marathon running. 2. Women runners.   I. Vilines, Alyce, 1956-
    . II. Title.
  GV1065.R54 2005
  796.42'52082--dc22
                              2005037092

Cover design by: Jennifer Pales
Front/back cover runner: Danielle DiVito; exercise model: Jordan Vilines
Book design Kathryn Palandech
Printed in the United States of America
Pendragon Publishing
32 Main St.
Park Ridge, IL 60068 USA
www.pendragonpublishinginc.com

To all the selfless souls on the sidelines of a loved one's first marathon.

To Regis and B.B. for standing six hours in pelting rain,

and to Eric for celebrating in it.

–Wendy

To Sammye and Ryan, whose strength and courage were my inspiration

and to Rick, Jennifer, Jackie and Jordan whose loving support and

encouragement were my wings.

–Alyce

contents

introduction

Although this book will take you safely from sofa to sidewalk and then on to the starting line of a marathon, it is really not a book about athleticism. It is a book about the importance of setting a life-changing goal, the splendor of the adventure along the way and the gifts that await you at journey's end. It is a book written by two ordinary women who embarked on a 26.2 mile quest that opened their eyes, changed their lives and painted their hearts with moments unforgettable. And it all began with one very simple step…a change of shoes.

It's a gender trait we all share—our love of shoes. It's most likely a component of that X-factor. Change may not always be something we feel comfortable embracing, but a change of shoes…now that's something worth talking about. Remember the magic Dorothy discovered in those ruby red slippers? That same magic is waiting just around the corner for you. From the time you bend down to lace up your sneakers to the moment you stand back up, you will sense it. Maybe the magic is in making that first deposit of courage when committing to this life-changing goal. Maybe it happens along the way, as you find yourself learning new lessons and gaining strength at every mile. Whatever the reason, our hope is that the marathon magic that starts with those shoes will carry you beyond the sidewalks of your neighborhood and outside of the enclave in which you find yourself so safely nestled. Our hope is that it will escort you to oceans bluer than you've ever seen, sunsets more fiery than you've ever imagined and limitless skies that invite you to soar.

As you wade into the pages of this book, whether timidly or at maximum speed, remember that first step is not with your feet but with your heart. And as Norman Vincent Peale so aptly instructed, "Throw your heart over the fence, and the rest will follow." It's time to start throwing, ladies.

Part 1

indecent proposal

"I could not at any age be content to take my place
in a corner by the fireside and simply look on."
-Eleanor Roosevelt

From Wendy's journal –

January 1, 2004

It seems only fitting that each of us start a new year off with a new attitude. So I am sitting in front of a computer screen with a fresh resolve to record my thoughts and feelings weekly as I begin one of my New Year goals—to run a marathon in the spring.

Okay, let's put this in perspective…a 43-year-old woman with an arthritic knee is going to train for and run 26.2 miles. To put it simply, it has always been a desire of my heart. Then one day this fall, as quickly and as magical as a revelation, the idea crept into my mind and refused to leave. It has been sitting there ever since, like a childhood Boogeyman loitering in the corner of a dark bedroom. I knew it would soon join the other skeletons in my closet if I didn't confront it. So I did.

I started praying for a running partner. God knows me better than anyone, so I surmised that if He wanted me to realize this dream, He would certainly help. Through a series of odd circumstances, I found myself joining the Team in Training with the Leukemia and Lymphoma Society. For the past few weeks, I have been giving God credit for leading me to this running group, but I realized just today that God did so much more for me. He brought me Alyce. And who would have imagined that He would bring me someone who not only runs at my same pace but dreams with my same passion. Additionally, who would have thought that learning how to run is in a weird, quirky and terribly exciting way teaching me how to walk.

chapter 1

what's in this for me? making a plan

one block

Our entire lives are tapestries woven by God, and I think none see their completion until death. How awesome is this thought. We are still growing, and changing and becoming. Threads spun years earlier one day take shape and reveal an intricate design.

I know this because 24 years ago I sat in a garden-variety classroom on a university campus and listened to a literature professor introduce herself. A tall, lithe woman with gray hair carefully laid out her plan to bring the works of Shakespeare to life. She told us her name, which I have since forgotten. And she recounted a personal anecdote, which was forever blazoned into my memory. She told the story of her divorce.

Becoming more and more a commonplace word in our society, divorce still leaves vestiges on each individual that are distinct and exclusive in their scarring. I could tell this from her face. Divorce had defeated her. It had surprised her with a meanness she had never known and blanketed her with a suffocating paralysis.

So one day this professor made a decision. She decided to take up jogging. As simply as that. She woke up; she went outside; and she walked around the block. One block. Each day thereafter she forced herself to walk around this block. I don't remember her entire process. I only remember that the day I met her she introduced herself not only as an English professor but as a marathon runner. A change of action… a change of outcome.

I believe her story was one of the threads in my tapestry. Just a beginning of a design. *Nothing* recognizable at 19. Just a knot and a stitch or two. But God knew what He was weaving.

Twenty-four years later I decided to run a marathon. I was no longer the impressionable young coed sitting in a Shakespeare class, but I nonetheless remembered the formula shared with me by this wise, seasoned woman. One block.

- Wendy

David Whitsett, Forrest Dolgener, and Tanjala Kole, the authors of *The Non-Runner's Marathon Trainer*, instruct beginning runners to take a rather unorthodox initial step towards making their dream a reality. "…start telling people about what you're doing. Each day tell one new person that you are a marathoner." Somehow speaking it aloud ferments the intention. Disregard the fact that you are a busy mom with lively children and carpooling duties. Forget that you are a middle-aged woman with an arthritic knee. Listen to your heart, and step out in faith. Start telling everyone of your plans to run a marathon, armed with the knowledge that you will be placing yourself at risk. At risk for laughter. At risk for skepticism. At risk for ridicule. Hold close Eleanor Roosevelt's advice, "No one can make you feel inferior without your consent," and tell the world of your plan. Take this tangible action that will prevent you from retreating. Put a voice to your dream; place yourself on that limb. Let others laugh; let others doubt. You've got better things to do…you have a block to run.

no more excuses

Once the seed to follow our marathon dreams planted itself in our hearts, we began to silently fret, giving birth to the many hundreds of perfectly logical reasons we couldn't possibly complete such an endeavor. A former smoker, Alyce doubted the ability of her lungs to endure the rigors of long distance running. Wendy worried about her knees. Casual jogging in years past left her joints slightly tender and swollen. Even now, when walking up steps, her knees creak louder than old wooden floors. After reading somewhere to ice the knees for 10 minutes after every run as a preventative measure, Wendy did just that. Whether they ached or not, she heaped them with freezing cold packs after every run, even one and two milers. And we were both religious with our stretching.

There will be bad knees and challenged lungs, stressful jobs and demanding households. Even if you successfully dismiss all the many excuses not to pursue your marathon dream, rest assured your friends, coworkers and family will provide you with their own lists.

The fact is this. All our worrying was for naught. Alyce's cardio-conditioning increased in text-book fashion, and Wendy's knees never failed her. Just dutifully follow your training calendar, as it will gradually coax your inner athlete to the surface, building muscular and skeletal strength at a safe and steady pace. The human body is an amazing machine and will not disappoint you. In fact, your body and the shape it's in today should not concern you nearly as much as your mindset. Don't waste your energy on self-doubt. There's a much better return on believing in yourself. Don't make excuses. Make plans. Make a difference. Make every moment count.

It is always wise to consult a physician just to set your mind at ease.[*]
Nonetheless, the most difficult obstacles to defeat are psychological, not physical.
Throw the excuses out the door with the trash. All of them. Clear you mind, lace
your shoes, and march onward.

selecting a marathon

In 1970, 55 runners completed the New York Marathon. Today, well over
30,000 participants cross that finish line, many of them women. In any given
month, more than 25 marathons are held in U.S. cities from coast to coast, as well
as half marathons (13.1 miles) and mini-marathons (usually ranging from 7 to 12
miles). Finding a race in your area should not be difficult, but don't rule out the
option of traveling to another city for the big event. Should you decide to train
with a charitable organization, they are often affiliated with or suggest specific
races. In addition, they usually take care of the registration and travel details,
and you have teammates to keep you company.

An internet search on any computer will bring up hundreds of
destinations from which to choose (and we all like options). If you're a west coast
junkie, consider the Rock'n'Roll Marathon and boogie through the streets of
San Diego alongside Elvis. If your style is more Stetson than surfboard, trot past

---

[*] The American Medical Association recommends that a person consult his physician prior to
beginning any new exercise program.

the Grand Ole Opry in the Country Music Marathon in Nashville. We happen to be partial to Cincinnati's Flying Pig Marathon, heralded by Runner's World magazine as "a textbook case on how to organize a major marathon." While some enjoy the edge they have on out-of-town participants by having the luxury of running portions of the course before the big day, others prefer entirely new terrain for their marathon run.

A little research will also provide you with invaluable information regarding course terrain and average annual temperature. If the bulk of your training has been in single digit temperatures along flat running paths, you might think twice about signing up for the Big Sur International Marathon along scenic but hilly Highway One in California. Perhaps the best advice we can give you is to be mindful not to select your marathon based solely on expected climatic conditions. Mother Nature is, at best, unpredictable and even geographic locations noted for glorious weather can often surprise you with unseasonable conditions. Be prepared for anything! Also keep in mind the benefits of running your first marathon within driving distance for family and friends who will undoubtedly want to be there to cheer you on. Check our Resource Guide for more ideas of races throughout the U.S.

You've set your goal, you've selected a race, now all that's left is to make it official. It's time to register. Yes, we know. This is a big step, and you haven't even begun your training yet (your thoughts exactly?) But this is your first official starting line. By typing in your name on that registration form and clicking "submit" you will have mentally clicked "commit." The race is on.

determining your strategy

Stop questioning the sanity of your decision to do this (your confidence will increase incrementally), and start strategizing the logistics. Running a marathon, if not a misnomer, is at the very least a broad term. You need not sprint like an Olympian to complete a marathon. You need not even run. In fact, the number of walkers participating in races today is growing rapidly. Your strategy can range from running to walking to a combination of both (even a little skipping if the mood strikes is considered acceptable). Mike Henderson of Deep River, Connecticut, ran the entire length of the 2004 Marine Corps Marathon in Washington, D.C…backwards! (Although it is a known fact that some mothers indeed have eyes in the back of their heads, this is not a strategy we recommend.) Your goal, however, as a first-time marathoner, should simply be to finish. At the end of the day, every fitness walker, race walker, jogger, sprinter and those doing a little bit of everything will earn the same title…marathoner. On race day, whether you feet are walking or running across that finish line, your soul will be dancing.

The training regimen provided in this book is for both walkers and runners. We relied upon the expertise of Karen Cosgrove, world class runner and seasoned marathon coach, to share with you the same training schedule she has used with over 6,000 first-time marathoners throughout her 15 years of coaching. "Keep in mind that you are not doing this to win the race," she explains, "Your only goal is to finish." The key is not your pace, but your consistency and dedication. Karen also advises, "Don't look at the big picture. It's about taking single steps…a day at a time."

As baby boomers continue to age, fitness walking continues to grow as the most popular form of exercise for Americans. This trend is reflected in the growing number of races that are becoming walker-friendly. In fact, nearly 40 percent of the participants in the Honolulu Marathon and the Los Angeles Marathon walk the distance. If you are lucky enough to enter either of these races, you'll find yourself keeping company with over 7,000 walking buddies in Honolulu and 4,000 in Los Angeles. Walking provides you with most of the health benefits of more intensive exercise while minimizing the risk of injury. We also must mention that in most races, walkers enjoy a one hour head start on the rest of the pack.

Many people follow a run/walk strategy officially known as the Galloway method, created by Olympian Jeff Galloway. Some athletes actually report faster times using a run/walk program such as this versus continuous running. They give credit to the planned walk breaks which allow the body to recover more quickly.

However, since your goal is simply to finish, you should find a run/walk combination that feels comfortable and repeat this cycle for the entire marathon. For example, we used a two minute walk/six minute run principle. Cincinnati's Team in Training coach Karen Cosgrove suggests a ratio of one minute walk breaks for every three to four minutes of running for beginners. Veteran runners, however, can customize a ratio more suited to their abilities. Even if you choose to run the entire distance, don't discount the importance of walk breaks.

Especially in the beginning stages of training, do not feel disheartened if you need to walk a bit. Our very first day of training (after we had told the world we were going to run a marathon) was a lesson in humility. We could not jog an entire mile. So walk if you must, jog when you can, and take solace in the fact that there will be others, somewhere in the world, even shuffling and waddling.

finding time

Another concern of many women is finding the time to train. Fortunately, there are several devices on the market that can help.

1.) **The treadmill.** Especially in inclement weather, the convenience of a treadmill is definitely a plus. Remember to adjust the incline from time to time, though. No marathon course is completely flat.

2.) **The alarm clock.** We hate to say it, but you will probably become well acquainted with dark mornings and the halogen glow of streetlamps. You may also be pleasantly surprised upon returning from an early morning jog at how amazingly energized you will feel and glad to have checked one item off your daily list.

(If you happen to be a mother, especially one of preschoolers, you may find the following items of particular interest.)

3.) **The jogging stroller.** We know you've seen them, an umbrella-type stroller with three funky wheels. Don't laugh. We've seen grown men in races pushing these contraptions up hills that we could barely climb unencumbered. They would agree that this is a great way to train while spending time with your child.

4.) **The husband.** (If you have trouble locating this item, check the couch.) When the weekend arrives, leave Dad in charge for a few hours. This strategy can pay off in several ways. Training time for you. Bonding time for Dad and the kids. And medical specialists will confirm the fact that children will not starve to death in two or three hours.

With thoughtful planning and perhaps even a little help from friends, making and taking the time to train is well within anyone's grasp. Be accepting of the fact that even well laid plans do occasionally get broken. Flexibility will be key. You may need to switch Wednesday's run to Thursday or even break up a long session into two runs of shorter duration (one before work and one after).

The bottom line is this. If you want to do something badly enough, you will find a way. This may require sacrifice in some facets of your life, but the pay-off is worth it. During our training months, we both found that weekend social events lessened, as we were too tired from our Saturday morning distance run. What did we lose? A party or two. What did we gain? So much more. Wendy still remembers the approving smile of her youngest son when she returned home from runs. He always greeted her at the door with ice packs.

"when" not "if"

Stop thinking in terms of "dream" and think in terms of "plan." Erase the word "if" from your vocabulary and substitute the word "when." Just as rehabilitating addicts depend on a litany of rules and strategies to break old habits, start changing your own modus operandi one step at a time. If you catch yourself uttering "if I finish the marathon," immediately rephrase, "when I finish the marathon." You will learn that this change of behavior produces an attitude that spreads beyond your training mindset and colors your perception of life.

let's go shopping

If you have maintained a respectable amount of skepticism so far, perhaps now we've won your full attention. Let's be honest. Isn't any excuse a valid one for a shopping excursion? Besides, we're only talking about three items, albeit essential ones.

First, you need a good pair of running shoes. We cannot stress enough the importance of this investment and the wisdom of doing it now. We both purchased our first pair of shoes from large sporting goods stores rather than smaller running/walking shops. These specialty shops, however, are usually staffed by experienced athletes or trainers that analyze your stride and fit you with the proper shoes adjusted to your foot type. We both experienced slight injuries later on that were quickly corrected by different shoes. You may spend a few extra dollars, but the best defense against injury is the correct pair of shoes. Make this your first purchase and your most prideful one. And remember to tell the expert behind the counter that you will be completing a marathon, not that you hope to. Turn ahead to Chapter 6 and read more about selecting the right shoes.

Secondly, you will need a comfortable, well-constructed sports bra. This can be found in many stores, from high end specialty shops to economically priced retail chains. The key is the fit and the fabric. Make sure it is synthetic, not cotton, as this will wick away moisture from your body. And take the time to try it on. Trust us, comfort counts. Once again, turn to Chapter 6 and read the section on sports bras before heading out the door.

Now that your body is fitted with the essentials, it is time to equip your mind. The last item on your shopping list is a rather unorthodox one—an inspirational daily calendar.

We gifted each other with small desk-top calendars soon after we committed to train for a marathon. We had both enjoyed such calendars before. You know them. A flip of the page (when remembered), some clever words. A peaceful adage in the middle of a hectic day. However, this calendar was different. This calendar took up residency in our homes a week after we told the world we were going to complete a 26.2 mile race. A week after we made a decision that mocked all logic in our worlds. And those daily verses and quotes became much more to us than momentary respites from loading the dishwasher. They became personal. A tutelage that fueled our shaky self esteems daily and reminded us that nothing of real value ever comes easy or by chance. So spend a few dollars on an inspirational desk-top calendar and start training your mind as well as your feet.

lacing it up

Hopefully by now you are on the path to believing in yourself. This first step, making a commitment, is the most important one you will take throughout your marathon journey.

- Tell everyone you see you are going to complete a marathon.
- No more excuses.
- Schedule a visit with your physician just to set your mind at ease.
- Plan your strategy. Learn about the run/walk options and allot time for training.
- Select a race and register.
- Change your mindset from "if" to "when."
- Make your initial purchases.

These actions alone have set you on a course that will change your life… all from a simple change of shoes.

one woman's story

When a soft spoken, reserved, middle-aged woman appeared one Saturday morning at a charity group training session, everyone assumed by her shiny SUV and well-groomed demeanor that her motives were surely philanthropic. And Dee Martin's purpose may have begun as a mission to help others, but somewhere along the jogging trails and sidewalks, it became her emancipation.

After 28 years of marriage, Dee's husband walked away from his enviable home, his suburban existence and his wife. In countless ways, this is many women's story. Four children, a manicured lawn and broken promises to show for years of commitment and dedication. But in other, quieter ways, this is Dee's story. A dedicated mother constantly devoting her life to her children, and a people-pleaser often following the dictates of others, she decided to take one distinctive step that she could call her own. One definitive action. One outrageous action. She decided to run a marathon.

Imagine a 51-year-old woman, with flawless make-up and impeccable clothes, who is more comfortable satisfying the stereotype of perfect wife and mother than donning a pair of athletic shoes. Imagine a woman, fighting to hold on to a diminishing self-esteem. Imagine a woman, afraid that she is only defined by others...and that one day she will cease to exist.

Dee unabashedly admits that she cried for a year after the collapse of her marriage. She also describes the afternoon that she ventured outside for a walk and strangely enough spotted her husband ahead on the sidewalk. She turned and ran, no more than a quarter mile back to her house, downhill at that. And, Dee explains, she "liked how it felt." She knows now that in running away from all the tears, she was running toward something better. Strength.

Dee's running continued in what she describes as her "mailbox strategy." On afternoon walks, she would challenge herself to jog from one mailbox to the next before taking a break. First one-fourth mile, then one-half mile, until she was able to jog three continuous miles. It was this catharsis that helped her deal with stress as her father underwent by-pass surgery. It was this mailbox strategy that also catapulted Dee into the midst of a curious group of diverse people, all clad in purple shirts and newly-purchased tennis shoes, known as the Leukemia and Lymphoma Society's Team in Training.

Dee came to that first meeting, and she clung to a sentence spouted by one of the coaches: "Some things are in your control, and some things are not. This marathon is in your control." Dee ran with it. Literally. A few months later, she traveled to Alaska to visit her son Shawn and to run in the Mayor's Midnight Sun Marathon. Shawn surprised her by running the 26.2 miles alongside his mother. Maybe it was the photo of four-year-old Jennifer (Dee's "hero") pinned to the back of her shirt. Maybe it was the thought of her 79-year-old father manning a water stop in 40 degree rain at one of her practice races. Maybe it was the realization of a truth her coach had preached continuously, that she was "not a cardboard cut-out." Whatever it was, Dee finished the race, just steps in front of her son and miles in front of defeat.

over the coffee cup

Dee's first marathon: The Mayor's Midnight Sun Marathon, Anchorage, Alaska

Age: 51

Time: 5:27

Q: Were you very athletic before you decided to take up jogging and later train for a marathon?

A: Not at all. I had never played any sports.

Q: What was the reaction of your friends and family when you decided to run a marathon?

A: Everyone was positive. After sending out letters to raise funds for the charity, I even received money from my landscaper, my plumber and dentist! I raised almost $7,000.

Q: Were you ever injured during your training?

A: Not really, but I did take two weeks off to let my body rest because my legs were hurting.

Q: What one thing did you do right during your training?

A: I followed the schedule exactly.

Q: What one thing did you do wrong?

A: I was not aware that I needed to do knee strengthening exercises until I saw a physical therapist.

Q: Did you hit the wall during the race?

A: At mile twenty I fell apart. I became very emotional, but my son encouraged me. Also onlookers started calling to me "You can do it for Jennifer…she's so beautiful!" That pulled me through, then I had a burst of energy near the end.

Q: Any advice for first-time marathoners?

A: Follow your training schedule. If you trust the professionals, no matter what shape you are in, you can do this. Nothing will make you feel as good. I felt like a celebrity when I finished.

Q: Any million dollar trade secrets?

A: Make sure you do strengthening exercises, and eat a steak each week for the protein. It will really make a difference in your performance.

chapter 2

misery loves company: training with a team

Partnerships can be of corporate magnitude, marital bliss, or even criminal association, yet all gain strength from the union of more than one body, more than one mind and more than one soul. Throughout our marathon training, the old adage, "there is strength in numbers," rang true for us. From the initial commitment to the finish line celebration, we knew that the key to our success was having a loyal training partner. We further customized our training schedule by participating in group runs on Saturdays, saving the weekday jogs for just the two of us. Whether your training partner is one close friend or a group of 30, the camaraderie will keep you motivated and accountable. There will be, of course, those who do not share this sentiment, preferring instead to use their training as quiet time. But for the rest of us who find ourselves strapped for time, training together can be an ideal opportunity for nourishing a friendship while simultaneously meeting a fitness goal. I think this is referred to as multi-tasking!

the company of others

Most communities have established running groups of all levels of experience, from the novice to the elite athlete. If your region does not, consider recruiting a group of your friends or neighbors to start such a club. Typically these groups meet one to three times per week and are divided according to fitness levels and experience. Even athletes who choose to train alone during the week may elect to join a group on weekends for their longer distance treks. Group training provides a perfect opportunity to exchange tips, stories and accomplishments with fellow road warriors. Whereas your friends and family may grow weary of your training sagas, running comrades will share in your enthusiasm.

Specialty running and walking stores are your best source for information on local running clubs. Pace teams, groups that train according to a specific speed, are one

> MEMORY JOGGER...
>
> "We were reminded of our middle-aged status the first time we showed up for a long-distance group run. Tiny strips of paper with street directions were distributed in case a straggler couldn't remember the route home. A lot of good it did us, as we couldn't decipher a single word without our reading glasses!"

example of such clubs. Not only do these athletes train together, but they can't be missed bounding down the course on race day with army-like precision and cadence, chanting and keeping each other on track. Teams for many different pace levels exist, from a 7-minute mile pace to a 14-minute mile.

charity teams

In addition, several training groups are focused around a charitable cause, such as the Leukemia and Lymphoma Society's Team in Training, the National Multiple Sclerosis Society's Making Strides Against MS, and the Arthritis Foundation's Joints in Motion. A more complete list can be found in the Resource Guide.

Joining a charity sponsored team provides you with running partners, a professional coaching staff and a chance to meet new friends. Mostly, it offers you a chance to look beyond yourself. You will be expected to raise funds for your chosen charity and in turn you are given the greatest motivator of all—the chance to run on behalf of someone who cannot run for himself. It is in doing this that your marathon journey goes beyond a lesson in fitness. It becomes a lesson in living.

Although all charity teams provide structure, the one we selected was the Leukemia and Lymphoma's Team in Training. Wendy attended her first meeting (alone), munched on the free snacks and wondered what on earth she was doing there. She even took the elevator to the second floor! Surely she did not have the body of a marathoner. But she learned later that she had something more important. She had the heart.

at arm's length

We all know people in our lives whose struggles are greater than our own. People whose names become euphemisms at dinner tables when 16-year-olds complain about curfews and siblings contest whose day was the hardest. In fact, the mantra of multiple generations has been "there are starving children in Africa…," but seldom do we remind our families about the man one block over who just lost his job or the church pianist whose son died in an automobile accident. All in our backyard. All at arm's length.

These "euphemisms" became all too real for us when we agreed to run the marathon for charity with the Leukemia and Lymphoma Society's Team in Training. The faceless people whose plights minimized our own suddenly acquired names. We met Lou, a retired gentleman with a crop of silver hair and a Santa Claus belly. He could not run a marathon himself because he was fighting leukemia. So we ran for him. There was Ryan, a nine-year-old whose soccer practices were replaced with radiation sessions. And there was Dave, who was determined to run this marathon because that was all he could do for his dying son. So he ran with passion, and probably hope and a humbling knowledge that he may outlive his child. These amazing people of steel and resilience…all at arm's length.

Wendy asked her sister-in-law, suffering from breast cancer, to be one of her official "heroes" for the marathon by sending her a list of "26 Reasons Why I Love You." She had an opportunity to interview Kathy.

I asked her a simple question: "What are three words in your current vocabulary that you never thought would be commonplace in your life?" I fully expected technical terms to top the list. Bone scan. Chemotherapy. Metastasize. What I never suspected was that an ordinary unassuming four letter word would be her answer. Hope. I came to realize that it was also her legacy.

Kathy is 53 years old and was first diagnosed with breast cancer 10 years ago. A routine mammogram did not reveal the growing malignancy in her breast, but in time all truths were uncovered. A lump led to a biopsy. Then cancer crept into her bones. A few angry cells exploded into a surreal existence comprised of needles, looming machines, medical jargon and sterile smells from still corridors. A life even a writer's mind cannot imagine. Truly only those members so cruelly recruited into this club could have any idea of its horrors.

When asked, Kathy shared details of her sickness. After a stem cell transplant, she lost every strand of hair on her body, even her eyelashes. Some patients lose their fingernails. She had to give away her pets. She had to drink through straws. And often at night she would sleep in a turban, so no one could see her baldness. "Bad hair is better than no hair," she laughed.

I asked about the turban. The scarf. Truly the perfect metaphor for breast cancer patients everywhere, I thought. The loss of hair represents loss of confidence, loss of dignity. I was wrong.

Kathy became more animated when she talked about turbans. "They don't represent loss," she told me. "They represent bonds. You see a turban and you know that someone else is fighting it, too." A strange melody of camaraderie in a cacophonous world.

Kathy has fought other battles as well. Her first marriage ended after 20 years. Her second marriage ended when her husband decided her couldn't live with cancer. Yet the message she shares with others is one of optimism. "Cancer doesn't have to be a death sentence."

My message is different. What I want to impart to others is that I am richer for having people like Kathy in my life, in my backyard. And I am grateful for the life lessons that training with a charity has taught me.

Kathy told me that she took scrumptious desserts such as banana pudding with her to all of her chemotherapy sessions to share with the

*other patients. They would talk and cry and encourage and laugh…
and eat. What a gift she gave to others! But she corrected me. "I always
came away with more than what I gave."*

Loving banana pudding the way I do, I find that hard to believe.

- Wendy

show me the money

Fundraising is perhaps the most daunting aspect of joining a charity sponsored team. For days after signing up with Team in Training, Alyce second-guessed her decision, intimidated by the commitment to raise such a large sum of money. But with a bit of guidance from the organization and one cleverly composed letter (tucked into her Christmas cards), she surpassed her goal of $1,200 in less than two weeks.

All charities will offer you tips and suggestions for fundraising; some even pay postage for your letter writing campaign. We have included in this chapter sample missives that worked for us. We find that one extensive letter writing promotion (aim for 100 people) is one of the most effective and simplest fundraisers available. We also learned that the percentage of positive responses increase proportionately to the state of physical conditioning of the sender. In other words, the more out-of-shape you are, the more money you can expect to receive. It seems people become enthusiastic at the thought of couch potatoes tackling a marathon!

You can become as creative as you'd like with your fundraising efforts. One athlete raffled off a quilt that his grandmother made at his workplace. Another charged his friends money for permission to write something on his race-day singlet, and still another to write messages on his body! Host a Happy Hour at a local pub, arranging for half of the proceeds to go towards your charity. Throw a dinner party and ask only that your guests bring a donation for the charity you're representing. You will be pleasantly surprised at others' generosity, and their support will emotionally fuel your mission as well.

Sample fundraising letter:

You may have already heard that... (you may want to sit down for this) I will be running in the Flying Pig Marathon in May on behalf of the Leukemia & Lymphoma Society. If you know anyone fighting a life-threatening illness, then you know that it is an everyday battle, much more challenging than one 26.2 mile race. I will be running this race to honor these people as well as my "hero" assigned to me by the Leukemia Society. His name is Lou, he lives near me, and unfortunately he is spending his retirement years battling for his life.

I have always wanted to run a marathon, but as I have become involved with the Leukemia/Lymphoma Society & have gotten to know many of the patients, I realize that this is not about me at all. It is about raising money for other people to keep living year to year, month to month. And it is learning that living is something you do not do selfishly.

Any amount is appreciated. Thank you so much!

Now, on a lighter note...

10 REASONS WHY YOU SHOULD DONATE:
1. Tax deduction
2. You want to be a part of saving a life from Leukemia
3. You are a generous soul & always give to charitable causes
4. You're a cheapskate but have decided to change your ways
5. I am your sister/sister-in-law/niece/cousin/neighbor/aunt's cousin's next door neighbor/etc.
6. You're invited to my house the weekend of the marathon & my best guest accommodation goes to the largest contributor
7. You have faith in me; if Oprah & Puff Daddy can run a marathon, so can I
8. You owe me money anyway
9. I have been participating in 6 a.m. runs in inclement weather without my make-up
10. You're hoping I won't contact you again for years to come

(This letter generated over $1,400.)

Sample fundraising letter:

Dear _____,
You may want to sit down for this one. I'm training to run a 26.2 mile marathon to benefit the Leukemia & Lymphoma Society!   It's true...run, walk or crawl, I plan on finishing the Flying Pig Marathon in Cincinnati in May 2004!

As I trudge through each of those 26 (don't forget the .2) miles, I'll have my sister-in-law, Sammye, in mind. Her courage in battling Non-Hodgkin's Lymphoma for the last two years has been inspirational. Her fight is far from over and yet she faces each day with a smile and renewed determination. I'm also running for Ryan Finck, the cutest little nine-year-old boy, who has been living with leukemia for more than half of his young life. Ryan has finished his treatment and will be considered fully cured in October.

My commitment to the Leukemia & Lymphoma Society, and to Sammye and Ryan, is to raise $1,200 that will go toward research aimed at finding a cure for these diseases.

Would you please join me in this effort? I can't make it without your love, enthusiasm, care and financial support. You can use the enclosed donor form and envelope to show your support (or disbelief!) Feel free to include inspirational messages, lucky charms and band-aids! I'll have you with me every step of the way.

Thanks, in advance, for your support. On behalf of the true marathoners, Sammye and Ryan, thank you, too.

Love,

Alyce

(With this letter, Alyce collected well over $3,000.)

lacing it up

- Recruit a friend or neighbor to train with you.
- Contact running/walking stores in your area for information on local running clubs.
- Consider joining a charity sponsored training team.
- If fundraising, remember to implement a letter writing campaign to at least 100 people as soon as possible. Include a self-addressed envelope in each missive.

one woman's story

We all find ourselves at certain crossroads in life, those palpable moments when we know that decisions we make can alter our life courses. Mine just happened to come the year I sent my second child off to college and my third into high school. Perhaps it was watching my three amazing young daughters move beyond me into a wonderful world of their own making. Some might term it a mid-life crisis; others might label it pre-empty nest syndrome Whatever the reason, whatever the name, I found myself looking for something to better define the part of my life that lay ahead.

My first foray into this personal search was an unsuccessful audition for the cast of Survivor. It was clear that my next step towards self-discovery would have to be one that put success in my hands, not in that of a production crew. And so it was that I found myself at a meeting of the Leukemia/Lymphoma Team in Training program, a group designed to raise funds for a worthy cause as well as to prepare people, such as myself, to accomplish an unfathomable goal… running a marathon.

I no sooner took my seat than I began to get cold feet…what was I thinking? Twenty-six point two miles! I began scanning the room for the nearest exit, when my eyes fell on her…the sweetest little, freckle-faced girl whose story her mother soon shared. Just six years old, she had battled leukemia for over two years. Her life had hardly begun and yet she was climbing mountains I had never even seen. My thoughts went quickly to my sister-in-law, Sammye, who at 52 was also battling cancer. In that moment I knew there was no turning back. I found the exit that night but not until I had signed the form that committed me to go the distance.

I was also assigned a "hero" that evening, a young patient who was fighting his own battle with leukemia and for whom I would officially run. Ryan Finck, age 10, just happened to be the Leukemia and Lymphoma Society's Regional Boy of the Year, and I felt honored to have been matched with him. The inspiration they all provided is impossible to put into words, other than to say that never, at any point in our five month training program, did I allow myself to entertain thoughts of quitting. There were many times I felt I had reached the limits of my capabilities, typically halfway up a steep hill or midway through an exhaustive run. At those moments, I envisioned Ryan and Sammye at the top of that hill, arms outstretched, willing me to take just one more step towards them. I never let them down…or perhaps it was they who never let me down.

We lost Sammye just 12 weeks before I completed my first marathon, yet her spirit remained steadfastly by my side, her name scribbled on an armband that encircled my wrist. At mile 23, a stranger ran onto the course and put her arms around my shoulders. She shared with me that Ryan had been hospitalized the night before and had called to let me know that he wouldn't be able to meet me at the finish line. At first I cried and then I smiled to myself. "Oh, yes he will," I thought, "He hasn't missed a run yet!" (Ryan learned that he was officially free of cancer on October 14, 2004.)

- Alyce

over the coffee cup

Alyce's first marathon: Flying Pig Marathon, Cincinnati, Ohio

Age: 48

Time: 5:28

Q: What was the reaction of your friends and family when you decided to run a marathon?

A: 100 percent supportive. Friends at work were always asking, "How many miles this week?" Although my husband was initially concerned with the largesse of my goal (suggesting a half marathon might be a more sensible objective), both he and my three daughters were my biggest cheerleaders, as were my mom and siblings.

Q: Were you ever injured during your training?

A: One month before the marathon, I sprained my ankle. My coach advised me to take one week off, so I did. It was magical, and I was back running the following week.

Q: What one thing did you do right during your training?

A: As a novice afraid not to do what I was told, I followed the training calendar religiously. After the race, I rebounded amazingly well.

Q: What one thing did you do wrong?

A: Too many bathroom breaks during the race! Having trained with a group, we were conditioned to stick together during our long distance runs. This strategy, however, had a heavy impact on our times on race day. Too much time was wasted as we waited in long bathroom lines every time one of us needed a break.

Q: Did you ever hit the wall?

A: No.

Q: Any advice for first-time marathoners?

A: I feel strongly about finding a partner or group with which to run. A partner will keep you accountable and fill the empty spaces on an early morning jog through the dark.

Q: Do you have a million dollar trade secret?

A: Be creative with your mental tricks on long runs. As a Catholic, reciting the rosary became my soothing mantra.

Q: What did you learn through this experience?

A: A million life lessons, many of which I share in this book. Most importantly it opened my eyes to a world of limitless opportunities and the knowledge that nothing is beyond my reach.

chapter 3

thelma without louise? training without a partner

running solo... with a smile

"Okay, I'm guilty. I'm a woman who will run alone. I do it despite the disapproval of my friends and family, my workers and my YMCA training partners. They always try to point out their fears to me: "It's sooooo dark out there." "What if (fill in your own horrible story)?" "Aren't you being stupid?" But deep inside of me, I believe that there is a fine line between living your life and living in fear. Hopefully, I will never be forced to cross that line. In the meantime, solo runs are a part of me.

Don't get me wrong. I love running with friends. I love sharing the ups and downs, helping each other get through the tough parts, and enjoying the easy parts together. Of course, I'm not just talking about running here, but life too. I look forward to the days when I'm not on anyone's schedule but my own. I set my own route—up my monstrous hills, five laps around the reflecting pond and one loop through my old neighborhood. That's my 10 miler.

You see, running is my escape and my challenge. My gift to me. I have solved lots of problems on a 10 mile jaunt. Just last week, I figured out my speech to the third graders at Elm Elementary, practiced my entire radio show (out loud) and redecorated my living room. After 21 years of running, this list is quite extensive.

People like when I'm running with my friends. And I do. Really. But not always.

Admittedly, any city can be dangerous to run at times. But it can also be dangerous to walk, drive and play. And sometimes I am afraid. It's human nature. So, I try to take precautions—like that Mace that I've been carrying for years. I've used it on a lot of dogs. Never a person.

Let me ask you...do you quit driving or flying because you fear an accident? Or never swim for fear of drowning? Or stop playing with your children fearing that you will throw out your back? I don't think so. I think that people believe that if they avoid certain things, harm will never happen to them. But guess what? Terrible accidents and crimes happen every day, everywhere, to everyone. The real issue here is how *much will you lose if you stop doing what you love. Too much, if you ask me.*

Anyway, if you see me running alone, please just wave. Then I will know that despite my "solo-ness," I'm really not by myself. Now I have you too...if only for a brief smiling moment."

- Julie Isphording, Olympic marathoner

alone but not lonely

Despite the increasing number of joggers dotting the sidewalks of just about any American suburb, you may find yourself taking to the streets without a running partner or group for many reasons. It is often a challenge to find a friend who is equally motivated, in similar physical condition or has the same "free time" as you to train. You may not have convenient access to a running club or training team in your area. And some women simply choose to run alone, grateful to parcel out a segment of their day with nothing to interrupt their thoughts but the rhythmic sound of their shoes against pavement and the soothing stroke of a cooling breeze against their skin. Sound peaceful? There are many athletes who swear by it (running alone, that is!) They will tell you it is the most productive time in their day, a rare opportunity to clear their thoughts, to plan their day's activities and to brainstorm ideas for a project at work. They will also share with you that running alone is an experience of heightened awareness, a chance to reflect on the beauty that surrounds us but is so often overlooked when distracted by conversation or life's hurried schedules.

Janet, a woman who found herself jogging alone after her faithful running companion moved away, was pleasantly surprised by the benefits of training solo. "Bonnie and I were often so immersed in conversation that we failed to appreciate the people and places we passed on our weekly runs. Now I find myself waving and throwing hellos to neighbors and acquaintances along my route…running alone has actually made me feel more connected."

safety

Whether you train alone by necessity or by choice, there are many strategies that can prove invaluable. Safety is among the most important considerations. Many athletes find themselves walking or jogging in the early morning or late evening hours. In this case, one of your best investments is a reflective vest, jacket or belt. These are fairly inexpensive and can be found at any sporting goods store. Although many brands of athletic shoes have reflective material on the back or heel of the shoe, the best visibility is offered by the clothing a runner wears. Light-colored or reflective attire advertises your presence to motorists.

A lightweight cell phone is another consideration, particularly on longer runs, and always carry some form of identification with you (ID shoe tags are a popular choice). Common sense will tell you to avoid remote areas if possible, particularly during the early morning or late evening hours. It is also wise, when training alone, to vary your route and the times of day that you run. Aside from the safety aspect of mixing it up, this will also work wonders as a boredom buster and can provide welcomed challenges as well as new perspectives. Don't forget to let your roommates or family members know the route you will be taking and what time you expect to return each time you leave the house.

Finally, if you are not sticking to sidewalks, remember to run against the flow of traffic. You are less vulnerable than when cars approach you from behind.

conquering challenges

In addition to safety considerations, training solo presents other challenges. For most, it will be the ability to stay disciplined and motivated. As with many diet or smoking cessation programs, "staying the course" can often prove difficult without a mentor or partner to urge you on and to help you stay on track. Without the sense of obligation accompanied with meeting a running partner or group at the corner at 6 a.m., you may easily find yourself sliding back under those warm blankets. This is when you will discover your daily training log to be a wonderful motivator (see page 83). Posting this log in a visible area of your home (the refrigerator or family bulletin board) not only provides you with a daily reminder of your goals and accomplishments but serves as a subliminal prompt to family members that you are "on a mission." You'll be rewarded with positive visual reinforcement each time you record your day's mileage on your log, much like the feeling of accomplishment derived from crossing off items on a daily "to do" list. And family members will be there to share in your progress.

If you are among those of us who appreciate more tangible forms of motivation, you might also want to set up your own rewards program. Consider gifting yourself with an official pair of running shorts, socks or even a new pair of athletic shoes after reaching certain goals. Exchanging last year's baggy gardening shorts for a sleek pair of running tights can work wonders in the transformation of your self-image…after all, you're an athlete now!

If self-motivation is simply not enough, enlist a friend to be your virtual training buddy, someone who checks in with you weekly to gauge your progress and listen to your running highs and not-so-highs. This virtual training buddy could be a coworker, neighbor, husband, child or even an e-friend you connect with on one of the websites listed in the Resource Guide. It is helpful to have an ally to listen to your training perils, but it is even more important to have a cheerleader to celebrate your triumphs. And go ahead and boast; you've earned the right.

Solo runners/walkers may also struggle with boredom or monotony to a greater degree than those who choose to train in tandem. As previously mentioned, many solo runners use their training time to clear their thoughts and to mentally attack problems that are difficult to think through in the workplace or at home, with their inherent distractions. This right brain thinking can effectively carry them for miles. There will be days, however, when your thoughts alone are not enough to keep you entertained for the distance and Mother Nature's attempts to inspire you fall short on that grueling uphill climb. This might just be the time to partner your runs with music. Many women swear by the elevating impact of music as they train, its ability to lift and carry them through their longest sessions with ease. There are a wide variety of portable music devices, ranging from CD and MP3 players to armband radio and cassette players, that allow you to rock while you roll. If there's a teenager in your life, he or she may prove to be your best resource guide. Remember, however, to save the higher decibels for your training sessions on indoor tracks or treadmills. When training outside, you need to be aware of your surroundings, especially when running alone.

Even the most seasoned and disciplined athletes can find those weekly long runs to be a challenge to accomplish solo. Sheila, mother of three young daughters, enlisted the help of her family during her Saturday training session.

Her husband, George, and the girls would set up water stations every three miles along her pre-mapped route. Once Mom quenched her thirst at mile three, her family would load up the Gatorade and gummy bears and drive to the next designated water stop. "The sight of all of them cheering me on at each pit stop did more to spur me on than the Gatorade the girls had mixed up the night before my run." Soliciting the support of family and friends is one of the best guarantees you have of reaching your goals. Their pride in you will translate into great motivational incentive.

A final strategy that may prove useful to the athlete who enjoys short jogs alone but prefers company for high mileage runs is to round up "relay buddies." You may feel alone in your endeavor to tackle a marathon, but it is usually easy to find acquaintances who are recreational joggers. Recruit them to share a portion of the distance with you. For example, run 15 miles with three friends, each accompanying you for five miles of the journey. Now is the time to be pragmatic, and more than likely, they will be flattered you asked for their assistance.

For women, finding time alone in their day can be a challenge, but more importantly, it can become an amazing gift. Whatever it takes to carve out that time for yourself will be well worth your efforts. Though you may not have a partner by your side as you hit the road, you will soon realize that you are never truly alone. Use this time to get to know yourself. Open your eyes, open your ears and open your heart to the music of the outdoors and the beauty that lies within you.

---

in someone else's shoes...

Favorite boredom busters:

> ➤ *"I am never bored, and I run almost completely on a treadmill, 22 miles/ week. I am my own best friend. Or maybe it's multiple personalities. Regardless, we all get along."*
>
> – Sally Young, age 52

> ➤ *"For my very long walks, I listen to audio books. So far, I've 'read' over 20!"*
>
> – Gail Frederick, age 42

> ➤ *"I sometimes choose a one way route to a friend's house. When I arrive, I visit for a while, then she brings me home. Somehow, anticipating my visit and having a fun destination in mind keeps me motivated."*
>
> – Ellen Tisdale, age 34

---

lacing it up

- Wear reflective attire.

- Carry a lightweight cell phone in remote areas.

- Carry identification.

- Inform family members of your route.

- Run against the flow of traffic.

- Post your training log in a visible spot.

- Reward yourself for achieving incremental goals.

- Enlist a virtual training buddy.

- Recruit relay buddies for distance runs.

- Vary your route.

- Consider music as a boredom buster.

Even if training solo is your preferred modus operandi, consider inviting a friend to join you on occasion. It may be just the spice you need to keep those running doldrums at bay.

one woman's story

Christian, Kendall, Jacob and Madeline only eat their broccoli because their mother does. And petite, fun-loving Jerri only eats hers to stay energized for marathon running. A doting, attentive mother of four (ages two, four, six and seven) heeds the wisdom of the following quote: "Don't worry so much about your children listening to what you say; worry about their watching what you do." So this young Chicago mother gobbles down her broccoli for her children's sake and she runs 26.2 miles for her own.

Thirty-nine-year-old Jerri d'Oliveira ran her first marathon nine years ago, without advantages of internet research or high tech gadgetry, armed only with a desire to accomplish a personal goal. It has been the races since then that have taught her the importance of "me-time" while managing a bustling household of spirited preschoolers.

Jerri awakens at 5:30 a.m. for weekday jogs, claiming that trading the loud atmosphere of a toy-strewn home for the quiet of empty suburban streets teaches her to listen. With an insightful smirk, she calls this her "focus time." However, she is ever-cognizant of "dipping into others' times." Questioned often by her peers about the time commitment her training requires, she refuses to feel guilty for the few hours carved out of each week for herself. She knows that it is because of her running, not in spite of it, that she can clean peanut butter smeared faces all day long with patience and grace. It is because of her running that she can show her children a mother that is healthy, strong and self-assured… a mother that cares about the reference point she gives her children…a mother that eats her broccoli.

over the coffee cup

Jerri's first marathon: 1995 Atlanta Marathon

Age: 30

Time: 4:14

Jerri's most recent marathon: 2004 Chicago Marathon

Age: 39

Time: 4:24

Q: What one thing did you do right during your training?

A: I psychologically trained for two weeks prior to the race. I kept saying "I think I can, I think I can."

Q: What one thing did you do wrong?

A: Lack of a proper diet. I did no research about nutrition. I didn't even eat pasta the night before.

Q: What helps you now while training with young children underfoot?

A: Joining a gym that has a babysitting facility.

Q: Any advice for first-time marathoners?

A: Do it for yourself, not for others. And in doing this, you will find that it becomes a gift to others.

Q: Any million dollar trade secrets?

A: I drink a Coke right before every long run.

chapter 4

get into the groove: components of training

a funny thing happened on my way to womanhood

We first met Karen Cosgrove as a running coach, wise and patient and always spouting words of encouragement. We have recently gotten to know her as a friend. A woman humbled by her own notoriety, unpretentious, with almost a school-girl eagerness to meet us on equal footing, secrets ready to share. And we can only imagine Karen as a youth. A little girl sandwiched into a family of nine children. Wearing the signature plaid of her parochial education, blouse untucked, learning cheers from her girlfriends on the sidelines while the boys sprinted across the field.

She dubs herself as a "pre-Title IX" child, a product of times when roles were clearly defined. Little boys fell asleep at night with NFL visions of winning touchdowns. Their pig-tailed counterparts, however, dared not dream beyond the kitchen, content to pack all their hopes into a "happily ever after" philosophy taught them by their mothers.

All this changed on a single day in 1978. Not at a bra-burning demonstration on Haight and Asbury or an anti-war rally on the Washington Mall, but at a street race in Terre Haute, Indiana. A quiet but daring decision transformed an unsuspecting 22-year-old girl into something she never envisioned being... strong.

Karen remembers that day with detailed precision. She tagged along with her brother's friends to the Terre Haute Marathon, intending to run a six mile race while they tackled 26.2. Fully aware of a woman's prerogative to change her mind, Karen did just that. She registered for the full marathon instead, although she had jogged no more than a maximum of six miles in her life. A curious thing happened. She finished the event in less than four hours. She then entered the race circuit, continued to train and within two years became an elite runner, ranking twelfth in the world in 1980. While other women found emancipation on college campuses and at women's rights rallies, Karen became liberated by a pair of worn out Nikes.

Eventually Karen became the twenty-ninth female out of 265 to cross the finish line of the 1984 U.S. Olympic trials. Unfortunately, only the first three finishers qualified, one of whom was from Karen's home town. Excited for her friend but disappointed in her own performance, Karen flew home that evening with the stinging irony that "the girl next door" was living what could have been her Olympic dream. Once the plane landed, Karen jostled through bands, flower bouquets and swarming reporters before she glimpsed her own celebration—an unassuming poster board sign held by her two-year-old son displaying the scribbled words, "Mommy, we love you and are so proud of you!"

Amazingly enough, four years later Karen tried again. Only seven months after the birth of her second child, she laced her shoes for the 1988 Olympic trials. Early in the race she stepped into a pothole and sprained her ankle, and at mile 11 she had to make the agonizing decision to drop out. The very next week her brother was diagnosed with a rare form of cancer and given only a 5 percent chance of survival. As many of us do when faced with heartache, Karen bargained with God to give her brother a second chance. She vowed then to "make a difference" with her life.

Today, Karen's brother is alive and so is her promise. She works with The Leukemia and Lymphoma Society, training ordinary people to run an extraordinary distance, a first marathon. In 13 years of coaching, she has guided over 6,000 people, most of them women, across that finish line. Her philosophy is simple. She keeps her charges grounded with common sense advice. "Listen to your body." (Having run over 90 marathons, she has never been injured.)

And not once has she asked anyone's race time. She believes that is not what's important. "It's all about making women strong," she responds.

We can't help but remember Karen's words when she first began her narration of this collage of memories. "A funny thing happened on my way to womanhood…" Indeed it did. And because of those twists and turns in Karen's road to independence, she finds herself today training more than just marathoners. She coaches women to be stronger than they ever imagined they could be. She not only gives them feet to run, she gives them wings to fly.

competitor or couch potato?

Although Karen Cosgrove's preparation for her first marathon (a six mile run being her longest!) is certainly not one we advise you to emulate, her attitude is. She proved that tackling 26.2 miles is 90 percent MENTAL. However, she also knows that not everyone reading this book is an active, 22-year-old. In fact, it is our hope that there are even a few self-confessed couch potatoes shuffling through these pages. For this reason, Karen, with her vast knowledge and hands-on coaching experience, has devised a training calendar to take you from sofa to sidewalk. If you feel you are not yet ready to plunge into week one of the training schedule shown on page 83, look over the following eight week conditioning phase and jump in where your capabilities will allow.

conditioning phase

	S	M	T	W	Th	F	S
Wk1	wts./ x-train	walk/run 20 min.	wts./ x-train	walk/run 30 min.	walk/run 20 min.	rest	walk/run 30 min.
wk 2	wts./ x-train	walk/run 20 min.	wts./ x-train	walk/run 30 min.	walk/run 20 min.	rest	walk/run 30 min.
wk 3	wts./ x-train	walk/run 20 min.	wts./ x-train	walk/run 30 min.	walk/run 20 min.	rest	walk/run 30 min.
wk 4	wts./ x-train	walk/run 20 min.	wts./ x-train	walk/run 30 min.	walk/run 20 min.	rest	walk/run 30 min.
wk 5	wts./ x-train	30 min. easy	wts./ x-train	30 min. hills	30 min. easy	rest	30 minutes long
wk 6	wts./ x-train	30 min. easy	wts./ x-train	30 min. hills	30 min. easy	rest	30 minutes long
wk 7	wts./ x-train	30 min. easy	wts./ x-train	30 min. hills	30 min. easy	rest	30 minutes long
wk 8	wts./ x-train	30 min. easy	wts./ x-train	30 min. hills	30 min. easy	rest	40 minutes long

patience

The hallmark of a truly great coach is his or her ability to inspire. Former decathlon champion and University of Michigan coach Ken Doherty stated, "A coach can be like an oasis in the desert of a runner's lost enthusiasm." In our opinion, sometimes the greatest leader is not the one out in front setting the pace, but the one beside you, offering encouragement. It does not matter how slow you are the day you walk out of your front door and begin your training. It doesn't matter the distance you cover, five miles or five yards. What does matter is your commitment to your dream and your willingness to practice patience every month, every week and every step of the way. In fact, we encourage you not to look ahead on the training calendar; seeing "16 miles" in print will only induce a panic attack and a wave of depression at the very least. Follow the schedule one day at a time and be consistent. Training properly to complete a marathon means allowing your body to adjust gradually to stress and longer distances, so in this endeavor, patience is more than a virtue. It is a necessity.

During our research for this book, we have met some amazing people and talented athletes. We've met women who could not jog a single mile without stopping but ran a full marathon one year later under four hours. However, the individuals from whom we learned the most were those who cared more about the examples they were setting than the records they were breaking, such as

Sabrina Bugay-Willis, whose story we tell on page 77. When there are moments in your training (and there will be) when you doubt your ability to reach your goal, be patient and trust the expertise behind this schedule. It has been designed to strengthen your cardiovascular, muscular and skeletal systems at a safe and gradual pace. So don't be intimidated when lean silhouettes in racing stripes dart pass you on the sidewalk. They, too, had a first day in sneakers. Remember that athletes truly worthy of recognition are those who, knowing they can pass you, are not too proud to walk beside you.

the long and short of it

The key to understanding this training calendar is a literal one, and learning the reasons behind each component will make your journey easier.

> **Easy** = walk or run at a pace that is comfortable
> **Hills** = map out a course that includes some hills
> **Long** = the longest distance and most important session of the week
> **Weights** = weight lifting for upper body strength
> **X-train** = spend time engaging in an activity other than walking or running
> **Rest** = use today to relax and to let your muscles recover

Easy. On easy days you should train at a conversational pace. Enjoy the scenery. Don't push yourself too hard. If you train with a partner, think of these sessions as more social than technical. They are sometimes referred to as maintenance or recovery runs, because their purpose is simply to help you maintain your current fitness level.

You will notice that the majority of weekday training sessions are calculated in minutes, whereas the long weekend workout is measured in miles. This is because the long run is the most crucial one of the week. Team in Training coach Karen Cosgrove sees women's lives becoming increasingly busier every year. Midweek sessions calculated in minutes ensures greater success with training, preventing beginners from becoming caught up in what Cosgrove describes as the "mileage syndrome." It is less intimidating and more attainable to fit in a 45 minute training session than a daunting 10 miler.

Hills. If you equate sprawling hillsides and rolling terrain with work, you are right, but the pay-offs of huffing and puffing up even small inclines are big. Hill training helps to build your quadriceps, some of the most important muscles to a marathoner. It also helps to improve your running economy (how fast you can run at a given level of oxygen consumption). If you live in a region where reflective yellow bumps in the road are the only hills in sight, you may have to reserve your hill training sessions for a treadmill, where you can inject occasional inclines into your workout.

When training on hills, there are several tidbits to remember. First, shorten your stride without necessarily slowing your pace. Stretching out your steps will only tire you faster. Secondly, use your arms to help propel your body forward. Lean slightly ahead and work those arms. Thirdly, make a vow right now to start viewing hills as a gift to your glutes. Approach each mound and rise in the road knowing that hill training pays off significantly in swimsuit season. Eyes downward, arms pumping, strides shortened and a determined mindset and you are on your way to becoming a stronger athlete.

Long. If you compare your easy session to coffee with a friend, consider your long workout as a marathon day of house-cleaning, when you take the phone off the hook, roll up your sleeves and get to work. This is the most crucial workout of the week, as it teaches your body to burn fat and your muscles to store glycogen. If your body learns to use fat as its primary source of fuel, you are less likely to "hit the wall" on race day.

The distance of this workout should never increase more than 10 percent each week, allowing your body to gradually and safely adapt to the stresses of marathon training. Each week your leg strength is improving as well as your resistance to fight fatigue. Your pace should be comfortable, as your goal is not to break any records but simply to finish.

In addition to the physical gains from these long distance sessions, there are also mental benefits. These workouts give your mind a glimpse of what's ahead on race day. Here is your chance to practice not only fueling your body but training your psyche. Rehearse the mental tricks discussed in Chapter 10.

Rest. You will notice that the weekly long run is sandwiched between two light days. The day before, do exactly what the schedule dictates—rest. The day after, try to spend a few minutes weight strengthening and perhaps some easy cross training. Cartoonist Sydney J. Harris commented, "An idealist believes the short run doesn't count. A cynic believes the long run doesn't matter. A realist believes that what is done or left undone in the short run determines the long run." Such wisdom for training…such wisdom for life.

need a lift?

We would like to tell you that we lifted weights and sculpted our bodies without fail several times weekly during our training. We would like to, but we can't. Unexpected phone calls, doctor appointments and school meetings all had a way of appearing in our datebooks. It's called life. Although we tried to squeeze in some weight lifting sessions, we weren't always successful. We encourage you to do better, because this component of training reaps worthy benefits.

Research finds that slight improvements in performance can be seen in runners who added weight lifting routines to their training program. The primary reason you should include this aspect in your training, though, is not to make you a faster athlete but a stronger one. Resistance training strengthens your muscles and the connective tissues that literally hold your body together, improves muscle balance, increases bone density and contributes to overall fitness. Becoming a fitter and stronger athlete will complement your running/ walking performance.

If that isn't enough, weight lifting also helps prevent injuries. For example, the two most common complaints of long distance athletes are sore knees and shin splints. Knee injuries can be prevented by strengthening the quadriceps (the front upper leg muscle), and the best bet for avoiding shin splints is to build stronger calves.

Hence, add at least two short weight lifting sessions to your weekly regimen. There are many options at your fingertips, from joining a gym to clipping exercises from fitness magazines. Whatever your strategy, be sure to include strengthening exercises for the following major muscle groups: upper body (chest, shoulders, biceps and triceps), core (abdominals and lower back), and lower body (quadriceps, hamstrings and calves).

If you are a member of a fitness club, a trainer can walk you through a simple routine. If you prefer to conduct these sessions at home, you need only purchase a set of hand weights from a local sporting goods store or retail chain. You may want to consider buying two sets, five pounds and eight pounds, for a more customized workout. We have listed a few of our favorite exercises, but refer to the Resource Guide for more direction on beginning a weight strengthening program.

- Warm up – Ten minutes of easy movement, such as jogging in place or riding a stationary bike, to warm up your muscles
- Upper body – Bench press (chest), dumbbell curls (biceps), dumbbell kickbacks (triceps)
- Core – Crunches (abdominals)
- Lower body – Leg press (quadriceps), calf raises (calves)
- Cool down – Ten minutes of stretching for flexibility

Resistance training also aids in weight loss, as it helps to increase your metabolism, for those of you who wouldn't mind losing a few pounds. We also feel compelled to mention a final benefit of weight lifting, albeit a less technical one—a more attractive upper body! Face it, if you're spending endless amounts of time carving sleek thighs and curvaceous calves with your running, designate a small portion of your week to building shapelier arms.

cross training

The term cross training simply refers to engaging in a physical activity other than your primary one (walking or running). This supplemental conditioning increases your overall fitness by working different muscles than those used for running or walking. It also builds some variety into your training schedule. Aim for two cross training sessions per week, and opt for activities you enjoy.

However, it is important to select activities that are non weight-bearing (do not wield extra weight to your legs and knees). Swimming and biking are both superb choices for two reasons. Not only are they non weight-bearing but they develop your hip flexor muscles as well. These muscles are the primary ones to carry you through those last six miles of the marathon. As you become fatigued during a long distance run, your form slowly starts to deteriorate. Your upper body becomes tense and your gait turns into a shuffle. It is at this time when strength training for the upper body and cross training activities which work the hip flexor muscles pay off.

Even if you have no earthly intentions of adding yet another physical activity to the running/walking regimen proposed in this book (and are silently cursing the authors), there may come a time during the next few months that you are forced to reckon with the concept of cross training. That is, if you find yourself suffering from an injury. Often the only way to heal an injury is to stay off your feet, or at least the trails. So while tendons mend and sore muscles rest, you will need to find an alternative activity with which to maintain your aerobic fitness level. Cross train. Trade in your sneakers for a neighbor's bike or find access to a pool and swim a few laps. Continue cardiovascular training while allowing healing time for your injury. It works.

in someone else's shoes...

Favorite cross training activities:

➢ *"Elliptical trainer two times per week."*
–Dory Schade, age 42

➢ *"I ran up and down my back staircase in between hauling laundry."*
–Mandy Nichols, age 28

➢ *"When time allowed, I sandwiched in a spinning or yoga class at the gym."*
–Susan Christman, age 33

In addition to rehabilitation, cross training also helps prevent injuries and breaks the boredom of a monotonous routine. Although the most common cross training activities for marathoners are cycling and swimming, there is no reason why you cannot be creative. Join your teenagers snow skiing one evening. Walk instead of drive to the corner store. One mother of preschoolers unabashedly admits that her cross training consists of running around after her three and five-year-olds!

form

Because habits can be difficult to break, we suggest that you start your marathon journey off with a clear understanding of proper walking and running form. Throughout your training, spend some time consciously focusing on technique. Maintaining proper form will make you a more efficient walker or runner.

Running. Why worry about form when running? Why not just lace up your sneakers and take off? You need to spend occasional moments concentrating on technique because form affects pace and the amount of energy conserved and expended. Proper running form is not something innate; it is a learned skill, so practice is important.

Bend slightly forward from the waist, keeping your shoulders relaxed, not hunched over. Bend your elbows at a 90 degree angle and loosely cup your

> MEMORY JOGGER...
> "Banned from running for two weeks due to tendonitis, I took my run-ning partner up on her offer to use the bicycle in her garage. We dusted it off, inflated the tires and I embarked on my cross training adventure with gravity. In retrospect, however, we agreed the basket and banana seat probably tarnished our 'marathoner' image."

hands. Be very careful not to overstride, keeping your steps light, not heavy. Most importantly, keep your body relaxed and fluid. Team in Training coach Karen Cosgrove credits a simple, albeit unorthodox, exercise for teaching beginners to relax. She instructs them to jog around a neighborhood loop several times while loosely holding a Pringle in each hand. This serves as a mental reminder to keep their bodies relaxed.

Power walking. Sometimes the medley of terms used to describe walking styles (power walking, aerobic walking, fitness walking) only serves to confuse us. Aside from race walking, which is governed by a specific set of rules, these terms all simply describe fast walking and incorporate the same technique. Beth Eidemiller, certified walking coach for the Cincinnati division of Team in Training, instructs novice walkers to "think tall and walk tall." Good posture is the key to efficient walking. Keep your head up and focused forward. Keep your shoulders down and relaxed rather than hunched up toward your ears. Bend your arms at a 90 degree angle and swing them back and forth, not side to side. Keep your hands in a loose fist and low, below the sternum but pointing up higher than the elbows. If your thumbs brush against your waistband during each stroke, then you know that you have the correct angle. Use your arms as pendulums; the faster your arms swing, the faster your legs will go. However, be careful not to overstride. As your foot lands, let it roll from heel to toe creating a lift-off for your next step.

Race walking. An Olympic event since 1904, race walking employs a specific technique, which can actually lead to disqualification if broken in official race walking events. Race walkers must abide by two rules: One foot must be on the ground at all times, and your support leg must straighten when the heel touches the ground in front of you and remain straight as it passes underneath your body (the knee cannot be bent). Generally speaking, strides are smaller than when power walking; and because this is a more efficient form of walking, the race walker does not tire as quickly. It is also not uncommon to witness race walkers crossing the finish line well ahead of many of their running counterparts.

Because race walking is a bit more technical than power walking, Eidemiller encourages beginning marathon walkers to first concentrate on walking efficiently and with good posture than on an official race walking technique.

a word about walking

Because walking is the fastest growing trend in marathoning, we posed several commonly asked questions to Eidemiller:

Q: Do walkers need to follow the same marathon training schedule as runners?

A: Because walking is a lower impact activity than running, many walkers think it is not necessary to follow the same high volume mileage weeks as runners. Not true. They should adhere to the same schedule outlined in this book, whether walking or running the 26.2 miles.

Q: Should a walker purchase different shoes than a runner?

A: Many walking shoes are made from heavy leather. When training for a marathon, it is best to wear a shoe that is designed for long distances, even if labeled as a running or cross training shoe. You also want to look for a shoe with a low profile heel. A heel that is too thick will not provide enough flexibility for the foot to roll easily from heel to toe.

Q: I see many walkers wearing waist packs or fuel belts. Is this necessary?

A: Because walkers generally take longer to complete a training session, it is important for them to stay hydrated. There are several options available, such as "CamelBaks" (water loaded backpacks) and waist belts. A waist belt is convenient for carrying not only water but snacks, keys and even a cell phone.

Q: What is the biggest concern of beginning marathon walkers?

A: Time! They are always afraid they will not finish the marathon in the official time allotment. I always clock their times in the beginning of their training (without their knowledge!) then again a few weeks later. Their speed always increases significantly as they learn to walk more efficiently.

Q: What advice or tips would you give a first time marathon walker?

A: Be sure to fuel yourself properly during long distances. I see many women who don't like gel packs but fail to boost their energy reserves with alternative snacks. Carry cookies, graham crackers or other snacks to munch along the way.

lacing it up

- If not yet prepared to delve into week one of the training schedule, follow the eight week conditioning phase.
- Avoid looking ahead on the training calendar; take one day at a time.
- A rest day should precede your longest run of the week and a light day should follow.
- Include two weight lifting routines in your weekly training.
- Seize creative opportunities to cross train.
- Concentrate on proper form.

one woman's story

We cannot share the story of Sabrina Bugay-Willis without first telling the stories of Amy, Elizabeth, Jeannie, Hollie and a medley of other women from Bedford, Virginia. It is difficult to stereotype this hodgepodge of ladies; they range from dental hygienists and YMCA directors to a cluster of stay-at-home moms awash in diaper changes and preschool activities. They do, however, share a common denominator—their belief that the best example they can set for their daughters, their sons, their husbands and their community is to be strong.

Who are these women? If you live in Bedford, you've probably spotted them—under floppy gardening hats, loading camping supplies into an RV, directing a church choir or pushing jogging strollers along the sidewalks. They go to work, chauffeur carpools of tousled-hair children to soccer games, and make it home in time to feed their dogs, cats, even hamsters. And every Sunday at 3 p.m. they gather in the church parking lot or school playground…and run.

Jeannie Craig, a mother of three, claims she had not moved her body since the P.E. requirement ended in high school. That is, until she joined a gym in hopes of losing the weight she gained from her second pregnancy. She still recalls those first 10 minutes on a treadmill as the longest 10 minutes of her life. As she continued her pilgrimage to fitness, she entertained a secret wish—to run a marathon. It took a twist in fate, however, to make it come true. Jeannie's sister told her about a woman named Sabrina who was forming a local running and walking group, Women in Motion. Today Jeannie still muses over Sabrina's contagious enthusiasm for the sport. "She made me feel like I could become good at it. When I ran five miles for the first time, Sabrina pushed my daughter in the jogger for the final two miles (which were mostly uphill!) I was so tired. She said we could walk if we needed to, but I managed to croak out, 'I will NOT walk!' She said, 'Good for you. With determination like that, you will definitely run that marathon.'"

Kelly, another Bedford resident, began running at the age of 23 and jokes that her daughter has clocked as many miles in her jogging stroller as she has in her Nikes. She, too, has filed away bits and pieces of Sabrina's acumen for future reference. "We are showing our daughters how powerful women can be" is her favorite.

And there are other women—Brenda, who bought her first pair of running shoes at age 40. And Hollie, who remembers her inauguration into the running culture as "no immediate love connection" but continues to lace up her sneakers and plough forward. She is also not afraid to look back. "With every step we take, every mile we run, every race we race, and every pain we feel, we do it together…whether it's in person or in spirit." Hollie continues to credit Sabrina for gifting her, for gifting them all, with this unorthodox and courageous alliance called Women in Motion.

Sabrina's husband Kevin understands this. He recognizes the depth of the friendships his wife made as well as the void she left behind, when she met an untimely death in October of 2002. In the 33 years she walked the planet, she concentrated on one thing—using all of her gifts and talents. She had the courage to dream, as she turned her idea for Women in Motion into a reality. She taught numerous women that running was an individual sport, with success measured by their own progress towards their goals. She told them winning is accomplished by having the courage to start and the perseverance to continue. And today, her students have remained true to that maxim. They continue, with loyalty, to recruit others into this magical circle of athletes, whether their pace is fast, slow or only beginning. And in genuine Sabrina fashion, they make each member believe in the words plastered across the organization's website—"A runner is real when she takes the first step."

So you see, in telling the story of this one woman, we have to mention many women. Lisa, a dental hygienist; Sheri, an occupational therapist; Bilynda, an 11-year-old cross country athlete; and Sara, who placed running a marathon on her mental "things to do before I die" list. And of course, Jeannie. Former concert pianist…turned runner…turned friend… to Sabrina Bugay-Willis, an unassuming young woman who taught Jeannie and a host of other gals how to play a flawless Tchaikovsky Concerto with a pair of sneakers.

Postscript: In October of 2003, on the one-year anniversary of Sabrina's death, Jeannie indeed completed her first marathon. She says she felt Sabrina running with her, whispering those same words from their first five mile run…"Good for you."

over the coffee cup

Jeannie's first marathon: Columbus Marathon

Age: 34

Time: 4:30

Q: When did you first decide to run a marathon?

A: I saw my sister run her first one at the age of 18; I announced I would be running with her the next year. (I finally did it, but it took a bit longer--13 years!)

Q: Were you athletic before you joined Women in Motion?

A: No. I am, by nature, a "lazy lima bean" as my athletic sister jokingly calls me!

Q: Did you experience any injuries during your training?

A: I suffered from posterior tibial tendonitis just before I needed to begin training, so I followed a very unconventional plan, focusing more on building the long run rather than total weekly mileage. A lot of people called me foolish, because they did not understand how badly I needed to run the marathon that Sabrina knew I wanted to do.

Q: What one thing did you do right during your marathon?

A: I paced myself well. My husband says it must be the musician in me, like a built-in metronome.

Q: Did you hit the wall during the race?

A: No.

Q: Any advice for first-time marathoners?

A: During long runs practice how you're going to fuel.

Q: Any million dollar trade secret?

A: Ice baths! I took an ice bath after every single run during my training, and the tendonitis never came back.

Running Log

	Day 1	Day 2	Day 3	Day 4
Date				
Distance				
Time		Week	1	
Path/Notes				
Date				
Distance				
Time		Week	2	
Path/Notes				
Date				
Distance				
Time		Week	3	
Path/Notes				
Date				
Distance				
Time		Week	4	
Path/Notes				
Date				
Distance				
Time		Week	5	
Path/Notes				

chapter 5

footnote for the experienced: taking it to the next level

"Only as high as I reach can I grow, only as far as I seek can I go, only as deep

as I look can I see, only as much as I dream can I be."

- Karen Ravn

How many times have we chosen security and comfort over uncertainty and risk? How often have we opted for the convenience and safety of the interstate over the uncharted roads of a scenic byway, chosen to dive off the low board instead of the high or elected to follow the crowd rather than the beat of our own drummer? In doing so, in playing it safe, we risk cheating ourselves of the pleasures of passionate living.

Many of you will come to this book with some degree of running experience and miles of wear on your sneakers. Chances are you've even participated in a few road races by now, and yet the ultimate road race has yet to be notched in your belt or checked off your life list. You are among the majority of recreational runners, those millions who have discovered the sheer pleasure and healthful benefits the sport provides but have not yet ventured into marathon territory, the high board of running. You have, in fact, cheated yourself of the most passionate of road races.

As evidenced by the large numbers of people who have chosen this sport as part of their regular fitness routine, running has long proven itself to be a beneficial, convenient and (forgive the oxymoron) fun form of exercise. As testament to its broad appeal, runners come in all shapes, sizes and levels of expertise. They also represent all ages, all sectors of society and varying degrees of commitment to the sport. Regardless of where you fit into this very broad spectrum of "experienced runners," your prior exposure to running will prove advantageous as you start down the road towards your marathon dream. And yet, it may also prove to be one of your biggest hurdles when making the decision to commit to this summit of running feats…but more on that later.

coming to the training table

So where do you fall into this non-exclusive, all-inclusive group of experienced road warriors and how will your unique background impact your marathon journey? You are likely to identify with one of the following three categories: the casual jogger, the seasoned runner and the competitive runner.

Note: These three types of experienced runners should not be confused with stages of a runner's development, but rather three distinct mindsets or levels of commitment. For example, a novice runner will not necessarily progress in sequence from jogger to seasoned runner and then on to competitive runner.

Our sole purpose in distinguishing between these three types of experienced runners is to better enable you to understand how your prior experience will impact your foray into the world of marathoning, primarily in the early stages of training. Whatever category you feel best defines you, as an experienced runner you will have a distinct edge over the complete novice. You have been introduced and are now acquainted with the many intriguing nuances of running. You have not only begun training your heart, lungs and muscles but have stumbled upon the puzzling realization that your first mile is often your hardest in a run. (Shouldn't it be your last?) You have learned that your strongest runs may not come after consecutive days of diligent training but after a week of relaxing at the beach. You have discovered there is no greater high than a runner's high and that toenails really do grow back. You may already have found that priceless friend who will join you for a run in the pre-dawn hours of your busy day and you have the distinct advantage of knowing that every day, every run will be different than the one before.

the casual jogger

Simply defined, this is the runner who, with any luck, can locate her gym shoes when the opportunity arises and make her way to the sidewalk for a bit of aerobic exercise. The casual runner is typically a less consistent participant in the sport, often allowing inclement weather, travel plans and more alluring social engagements to pre-empt her running plans. Jogging is perhaps a healthy supplement to her fitness routine and/or a convenient social outlet easily squeezed into her busy day.

Many casual joggers, however, can find themselves stuck in a runner's rut, locked into a set pattern of running. They jog the same route each time out and they rarely log more than a set number of miles, typically less than five. They are unlikely to spend time stretching before or after a run or concern themselves with the latest in running footwear or attire. The casual runner may have even participated in a handful of local road races but shows little interest in pushing herself beyond the limits of her physical comfort zone.

First introduced by New Zealander Arthur Lydiard, jogging quickly gained popularity in the seventies as a means of building cardiovascular fitness. What began as a conditioning program of long, slow runs for competitive male athletes soon revolutionized the sport of running for all. Over the next three decades, as Americans developed a heightened and enlightened awareness of the need for a healthy lifestyle, there was a marked increase in the number of women who also chose to take their exercise to the road. In this once male-dominated sport (can you picture Donna Reed or June Cleaver in running shorts and a sports bra?), women quickly made their presence known…on the sidewalks, running trails and streets of America's communities. Many of these female pioneers began as joggers. In fact, there was little reason to stretch their limits beyond jogging as women were often not welcomed participants in competitive events. (Remember Kathrine Switzer, the woman whom a race official attempted to remove from the 1967 traditionally all-male Boston Marathon?)

Today we find the sport catering to this booming population of recreational runners and many races specifically geared to the female sector. And yet, the non-competitive jogger continues to make up the bulk of our female running community. Admittedly, their sheer numbers are perhaps the greatest incentive for the potential runner that lies in each of us, their non-threatening presence an invitation to those of us who feel intimidated by more elite athletes.

As a casual jogger, you bring to the table a level of exposure to running that can prove beneficial, particularly within the first few weeks of training. That period of time is perhaps the most crucial in terms of making an emotional commitment to your marathon goal. Your experience, however limited or inconsistent, will give you an edge of confidence over the complete beginner and may be just the extra boost of self assurance needed to get past that initial self-doubt.

Your body is also more familiar with the predictable increase in heart rate and breathing that accompanies exercise, a less than comfortable experience for the complete novice. Nonetheless, our recommendation is to begin with the conditioning phase presented on page 63. Depending on your level of fitness, choose to begin your conditioning at a point where you feel most comfortable. For some, this will be at the very beginning of the eight week phase, for others halfway through. Be patient during this time and realize that the foundation you build now will serve you well in the months to come.

Finally, consider joining a running club or group with whom you have common ground. Training with a cluster of friends, also first-time marathoners, will provide you with structure and incentive. It is no surprise that first-timers who train with a group, especially a charity team, are less likely to give up when the going gets tough. Surround yourself with positive people who will fuel your determination and help you stay disciplined.

During the initial runs with our training group, we (as novices) watched with envy the relaxed smiles and easy strides of our more experienced teammates. As our hearts pounded and we struggled to catch our breath, our minds filled with self-doubt and the fear of being left behind…we never were.

Months later, when our pace improved and we began to pass some of these same runners, we returned the favor, always checking back over our shoulder to make sure the stragglers were within our sight.

the seasoned runner

This runner is often a former jogger who underwent, perhaps unwittingly, a transformation along the way. This change is most apparent in her attitude towards the sport. No longer is running a fair-weather endeavor. Rather, it has become a respite from her fast-paced day, a much anticipated escape, a necessary part of her daily and weekly routine. This transformation often occurs as a consequence of the runner's rut in which the jogger can find herself immersed. Boredom with the same monotonous routine may prompt her to increase the length or speed of her run, join a running club, subscribe to running magazines or map out new routes to explore. Soon she finds herself sharing the exhilaration of a recent run with a friend at work or packing her sneakers in her vacation bag. She begins taking the time to stretch properly and develops a keener interest in her nutritional needs, understanding the impact both will have on her performance. As others look forward to putting their feet up at the end of a long day, she can't wait to put hers down (on the road) and let the pressures of life melt away as she heads out on her run. Most telling is the moment that she hears herself utter three simple but very defining words… "I'm a runner." They, in all their simplicity, are an inner acknowledgment and a public announcement that this sport has become an integral part of who she is. Her running has become more than a fitness goal or a social outlet; it is now her strength, her escape, and part of her identity.

It is important to mention that this transformation from jogger to runner does not always translate into faster speeds or longer miles. It is primarily a change in perspective, a mental evolution that makes one a runner in every sense of the word. On the other hand, so often this rebirth is conceived in the runner's desire to pick up her pace or to notch up her fitness level. For this reason, most women who uncover the "runner within" will continue to find new ways to enhance their running experience and to improve their performance. If nothing else, the transformation will find them taking to the streets whenever they can find a minute (and even when they can't!)

As a seasoned runner you have a clear edge over your novice and your casual running mates. You have developed a passion and commitment that will carry you gracefully through the early months of training. Your devotion to the sport has increased your awareness of the importance of proper nutrition and stretching. These two facets of training alone will give you a stronger start than your less experienced comrades. Consistency with your cardiovascular and muscular conditioning has paid off, allowing you to spend these early weeks of training embracing the mental challenges ahead.

Although the seasoned runner is not new to the world of fitness, she may be less familiar with the mental component of marathon training. The schedule mapped out for you in this book will provide the structure necessary to carry your body across the finish line, but your mental fortitude during that journey is essential to your success. Acquaint and familiarize yourself with the mental tips and tricks discussed in Chapter 10 and give them the same respect that you give to your physical training. You will learn to rely on your mind to pilot you through stretches of fatigue that can sideline the less mentally prepared runner.

Despite your clear physical advantage over the novice and the casual jogger, we still encourage you to begin your marathon training with the last two or three weeks of the conditioning phase shown on page 63. These preliminary weeks will instruct you to incorporate cross-training, a vital element, into your weekly training regimen. As the perfect complement to running, cross-training helps to strengthen less used muscle groups, allows overworked muscles to recover and improves your overall endurance. This abridged conditioning phase is certainly optional for the seasoned runner who has already discovered the benefits of supplementing her running with other fitness activities.

the competitive runner

This is the runner who has chosen to take her running to another level...
and then another and perhaps another. Her motivation lies in consistently
pushing herself to go beyond her personal best. This goal-oriented gal loves
nothing more than a challenge. Whether it's increased speed, distance or
difficulty, she's determined to reach the next level with each consecutive race.

In contrast to the seasoned runner, who enjoys the exhilaration of the
occasional friendly competition, the competitive runner lives to compete. She
will map out a year's worth of races and look forward to each one as though it
were her first. The free race day t-shirts and medals are still welcomed but not
as prized as a record-setting finish time. She will know how many miles are left
on her shoes and will treasure her sports watch more than the silver bracelet she
wears on the same arm. Her vocabulary includes such peculiar terms as fartleks,
intervals, PRs, splits and bonking, leaving her NRF (non-running friends)
clueless as to her native language. The competitive runner has learned to position
herself advantageously at the starting line, at or in front of her expected pace
marker, in contrast to her less competitive peers who concern themselves more
with lining up next to friends. (The competitive runner will arrange to meet her
friends after the race.)

The competitive runner is clearly a step ahead of her less disciplined and experienced running comrades. You may identify with this profile if you have already discovered the joy of participating in organized running events. You are confident and goal-oriented and have likely entertained the notion of running a marathon at least once. Your body and mind have been trained to call upon reserves of fortitude that less competitive runners have yet to discover. You've accrued a running wardrobe, a taste for high carb gels and a drawer full of medals. And yes, your friends have long since grown accustomed to seeing you sprint past them as they wait patiently in their cars for the light to change.

As a competitive runner, the advantages you have as you approach the marathon starting line are obvious. A surprising disadvantage, however, may be the very thing that defines you as a runner—your competitive spirit. Accustomed to achieving personal bests with each race, you may worry that your marathon performance will be less than stellar relative to shorter events you have run. Quite the contrary. Completing a marathon will the THE crowning performance of your running career! Although a competitive spirit is a healthy trait, your focus should be on finishing rather than setting any personal records. It is perfectly acceptable to aim for a target finish time (based on your performance in training), but make that goal a reasonable one that allows you to enjoy the race for the endurance effort that it is. Learn to pace yourself (remember the tortoise?)

and save that competitive energy for subsequent marathons or races of shorter distance.

You may choose to bypass the conditioning phase of our training program altogether, considering your current level of fitness. It is also likely that the first several weeks of the training calendar may fall short of your current running status. Keep in mind that this program is designed to take a runner from sofa to sidewalk to finish line. If you are already racing down that sidewalk, jump in at the point where you feel most comfortable and where your capabilities allow. Just remember the early weeks and months of training are designed to give you the firm foundation you will need for the more arduous training ahead.

on to the finish line

Regardless of your level of commitment to the sport, you may have at some point toyed with the idea of running a marathon. Perhaps you quickly dismissed it from your mind, discarding the notion as outrageous, senseless or unattainable. You may have a ready cache of pat excuses for the friends that ask you if you ever have or ever would embrace such a challenge: "My knees won't take me more than five miles…I just don't have the time…I could never run a marathon—four miles is my limit!"

In this chapter we have asked you to define yourself as a runner. We now ask you for deeper personal reflection… are you a dreamer or a doer? If that notion of one day completing a marathon creeps into your thoughts from time to time, don't dismiss it. Listen to that voice inside, throw caution to the wind and prepare to head down a path of incredible fulfillment. The same intrigue that first willed you to lace up a pair of sneakers and venture out your door is the same passion that will take you even farther...across that finish line which will forever cement your membership in that ultimate fraternity of athletes who were not afraid to chase their dream...marathoners!

lacing it up

For the casual jogger:

- Start varying your running route and make a commitment to stretch after each session.
- Begin with the eight week conditioning phase on page 63; jump in where you feel most comfortable.
- Consider joining a running group or club for structure and incentive.

For the seasoned runner:

- Pay as much attention to the mental component of training as the physical.

Start incorporating mental training into your routine by practicing the mental tricks discussed in Chapter 10.

- Begin your marathon training with the last two or three weeks of the conditioning phase on page 63.

- If you have not already done this, begin incorporating cross-training into your routine.

For the competitive runner:

- For your first marathon, your focus should be on simply finishing rather than setting any personal records. If you have a target finish time in mind, be realistic; this is a test of endurance, not speed.

- Jump into the training schedule outlined in this book at the point where you feel most comfortable. Concentrate on pacing yourself.

Part 2

what not to wear

**"Opportunity is missed by most people
because it is dressed in overalls and looks like work."
–Thomas Edison**

From Wendy's journal -

January 6, 2004

What is the number one lesson I want to share with my children about marathoning? To answer this, I have to ask myself what is the lesson I want to learn from it.

As sentimental as it sounds, I have hopes of this experience becoming a reference point for my sons. One day, when they are young men in a grown-up world governed by fortuity and happenstance, they can recall this race their mother ran and know that they too have the ability to conquer all kinds of challenges they meet. They can run their own races down the path of life and not surrender to a rock in the road or a hill that's too steep.

So, what have I learned so far? Aside from breathing techniques and the wonders of Ibuprofen, I have learned not to determine my dreams according to the faith of others. Most of my friends and family have been supportive, but a few along the way have not been very adept at masking their doubts. I guess it is a lesson that I knew all along, but isn't it comforting and easy to let others hold us up? Their hands are strong, whereas mine may quiver; their views are clear whereas mine may be hazy. But oh, when I finally stand by myself, I can see for miles...

chapter 6

nike doesn't come in fuchsia? injury prevention

running gear

When I was 20, I owned a pair of pink Nikes that cost $50, no small change for a college student in 1980. I took up running, probably as a fashion statement. Admittedly, I also wore a matching pink bandana tied across my forehead. (Let's hope that trend faded with the break-up of the Grateful Dead and will never resurface, along with wire frame glasses so large they could be fitted with windshield wipers.) I ran through campus. I ran to clear my head. I even ran to a bar once to meet friends. Ah, the independence gifted to me by those pink sneakers.

More than two decades later, amid needy teenagers and dishwasher loadings, when a craving to hit the sidewalks once again came upon me, I discovered the world of running had changed. Just as pregnancy demands a whole new wardrobe, so does jogging. That is, if you want to be taken seriously. And ladies, 100 percent cotton sweats riding up your derriere won't get you taken seriously.

Subsequently, I conducted ample research of sports fashions among a diverse sampling of twenty-somethings (the style-setting generation) from various geographic locations. I scanned university campuses, probed coffee shops, and even assessed the attire of those seven-foot-tall ectomorphs exiting the doors of specialty running stores. Three fashion revelations were universal among the more serious-minded athletes.

To begin, I learned the runners' creed—synthetics only (i.e. cotton is out). Secondly, as I wouldn't wear white linen pants to a summer bash with my panty lines showing, I've learned not to subject the fashion-conscious few out there pounding the pavement to this same debacle (i.e. lose the undies if wearing body-hugging lycra or spandex). Finally, I also learned not to look too coordinated (fashion-wise that is—you can never look too coordinated athletically!) Once in a while, I purposely throw in a brown and yellow racing top with my favorite navy shorts just to project the image of a "real" runner, at times too busy to worry over details.

So, with my new declaration of fashion decrees implemented, will I once again become that 20-year-old girl with the world at her fingertips dashing through the streets in pink Nikes? In spirit, you bet.

– Wendy

It is said that experience is the best teacher, so although we have gathered plentiful research from the experts on what a marathoner-in-training should wear (and not wear), it is our "trial and error" methodology from which you will probably glean the most information. Let's face it. We often spot a fashion "do" that we make mental notes to emulate, but it is the fashion "don't" we swear on our grandmother's grave never, ever to execute. We only need to see a size 20 woman wearing her size 6x daughter's tube top on a roller coaster at Six Flags once to convince us that it is not the fashion statement we want to make. So trust us as we tell you what items to wear, what items not to wear, and what items to immediately burn.

if the shoe fits

For simplicity's sake, we will start from the bottom up, working our way from toes to head. Besides, as shoes are the most important piece of attire needed to train for a marathon, we cannot stress enough the importance of purchasing a well constructed pair which properly accommodates your foot type. The best way to ensure that you are fitted in the correct style is to locate a specialty running/walking store in your area. More than likely it will be staffed by experienced athletes or trainers that will offer you more than just friendly service. They will analyze your stride, determine your foot type and suggest the best shoe for your needs.

There are five general categories of sneakers: motion-control, stability, cushioned, lightweight and trail. Athletes who overpronate (their feet land on the heel then tend to roll inward with each stride) most likely need the durability and rigid support offered by a motion-control shoe. Orthopedic insoles may also be helpful. These, too, are available in specialty shops. Stability shoes offer support along with a fair amount of cushioning and are usually good choices for average sized runners with normal arches and no severe motion-control problems. Athletes with high arches and underpronators tend to perform best in highly cushioned shoes with soft midsoles. For more specialized tasks, lightweight training and trail shoes are available. These are appropriate selections for the more advanced runner or elite athlete, not the beginner.

Once again let us stress the importance of seeking advice from the experts. Because females tend to have shorter, wider frames than their male counterparts, they also tend to overpronate. Consequently, they should be fitted with stability shoes…or should they? What about that lucky gal who is doubly blessed with her grandmother's gift of bunions? Perhaps your second toe is longer than your big one (a sign of intelligence, by the way). Fortunately for today's athletes, the process of determining the correct shoe fit for a specific need has become a science and is more sophisticated than ever. Seek the experts and trust their knowledge.

There are varying opinions as to how long a shoe lasts. According to Brad Dunlevy, owner of Meters & Miles Run & Walk shop located in Covington, Kentucky, a general rule of thumb is 500 miles or six months. It is not uncommon for an athlete to go through two pairs of sneakers when training for a marathon. In fact, it is better to break in a new pair before foot problems occur.

sock it to me

Obviously, the next article of clothing you will need is a comfortable pair of socks. This is truly a matter of preference, and only you can determine the type you most like. Just remember that we are not a "one size fits all" society, especially when it comes to feet. If you have small feet, wearing socks that are too large will cause bunching and perhaps even lead to blisters. Also, don't fall into the trap of thinking thicker is always better. Extra cushioning is not needed if wearing the correct shoes. Heavy socks can be cumbersome, and too much restriction can actually cause pinched nerves.

Experiment. Don't be content wearing the first pair of athletic socks you grab from your drawer. It may be worth your time to at least scan the sock racks in the closest sporting goods store, as you will be surprised by the variety in design. You may even become very much attached to a particular brand. Some prefer the air-conditioned quality of a thin, mesh pair designed for summer running, whereas other swear by the sheer comfort of soft, cushion-soled Thorlos®. And if you are initially hesitant to pay $14 for two things to slide on your feet, you will see it as your best purchase yet when you find yourself rummaging through dirty laundry because you "can't run in anything else."

We must add a final postscript to our sock expertise—synthetic fabrics only, as socks made from cotton will not wick away moisture. They can also cause your feet to sweat and encourage blisters.

keep it short

Before we hail all the nifty shorts and pants available to runners and walkers, we must address the topic of fabric. Once again, remember the word synthetic, as it is one of the sacred tenets of marathoners and a key word in choice of fabrics for shorts and pants. Natural fabrics such as wool or cotton absorb sweat. Synthetic fabrics do not. In fact, they wick moisture away from your body, keeping you cool on sultry days and dry and warm on cold ones. We know, synthetic is synonymous with polyester, and we all know the images that conjures up. However, today's synthetic attire is not the textile of the sixties, whose only redeeming attribute was no ironing. Today's synthetic is a high-tech sportswear which comes in a bewildering array of colors and designs. So let's get this straight. Although we are not advocating taking your morning jog in the lime green pant suit hanging in your closet since 1975, the sad chick who does this would at least earn points for correct fabric choice!

Having said this, there are several brand names for clothing with wonderful wicking qualities, but perhaps the most popular, accessible and affordable is Coolmax®. This line is carried in many moderately priced chains and allows you to save money on your everyday training gear while treating yourself occasionally to a sleek racing outfit from a specialty shop. Dri-Fit®, Polypro®, Thermax® and Supplex® are additional names to look for when shopping for lightweight, performance attire.

For warm weather training, athletic shorts come in a variety of styles. Traditional nylon tricot shorts have a silky shell with a built-in liner and an inside key pocket. These are lightweight and breathable and come in varying lengths. Marathon or long distance shorts are similar but have roomy triple back pockets for carrying gels, snacks and other items. If you prefer a snug fit, yoga and exercise shorts made from lycra or spandex are good choices.

When temperatures drop, shop for a pair of lycra running tights or, for the more modest athlete, a pair of comfortable, water-resistant wind pants. These can always be layered over tights or long underwear for single digit days. And it must be noted that even underwear has been reinvented. Under Armour®, a line of high-tech underwear that means business, is phenomenal. It keeps you dry, warm and unencumbered.

Check our Resource Guide for online stores which carry athletic apparel.

the sports bra

This item of clothing deserves special attention, because it is not just a bra but *the* bra—the bra that will provide you with more support than a stadium full of cheerleaders. And believe us, during a 14 or 16 mile trek, this is the kind of support you need.

This is one item for which cost should not be an issue. Drive to a specialty running/walking store, try on whatever sports bras they have in stock, grit your teeth and pay the clerk. You only need one, so splurge on a well-constructed, high quality design that is made from (you guessed it) a synthetic fabric. For A and B cups, a compression style bra, which keeps your breasts close to your chest, works well. For larger sizes, a harness design with defined cups works better.

Lastly, certified walking coach Beth Eidemiller stresses that walkers as well as runners need to invest in a comfortable athletic bra, especially to prevent chafing.

Forget the lycra... Nina Barough did. The only thing on her mind one morning in 1996 was transforming her brassiere into a flashy, feathered piece of art. Then she was going to wear it... while walking the New York Marathon! This one outlandish notion prompted Nina and 12 other women to power walk those 26.2 miles to raise money for breast cancer. With no experience in fundraising or power walking, and no direct knowledge of anyone with breast cancer, Nina raised more than just a few eyebrows that day. She raised over £25,000 and planted the seed for what would become a dynamic, worldwide charity raising funds for breast cancer research--Walk the Walk. Ironically, Nina herself later became a breast cancer patient. Today, the organization she founded continues to raise funds and awareness, and groups of bra-baring women continue to walk, with each step breaking new ground.

top that

As with pants, you should shop for tops that are also made from synthetic fibers. There are a variety of styles, so hunt for one that is comfortable and practical. We find a sleeveless top with a built-in sports bra is convenient. It is cool for summer training, and as temperatures lower, just toss a thin, long-sleeved shirt over it. You can add more layers as needed. Fleece pullovers are one popular option; and a lightweight, water-resistant jacket is an integral piece of every marathoner's wardrobe. One with numerous pockets is especially invaluable. It can also be tied around the waist when not needed, a technique which offers an added benefit…it provides a camouflage for those of us with less than perfect derrieres!

Finally, it may take a few extra minutes, but always try shirts on before purchasing them, as comfort should be your main concern. In the privacy of the dressing room, pump your arms as you would for walking or running. Is the shirt binding or does it allow unencumbered movement? There's nothing worse than running or walking for several hours in a too snug collar or a zipper that pinches.

"weather" you like it or not

Learning to dress correctly for the elements is a trial and error experiment. Besides the weather station, your most useful tool will be your running log. If you record the weather and the way you dress for your walks/runs, in a short amount of time you will know exactly which shirt, which jacket and which accessories are needed for different temperatures. A wonderful rule of thumb when beginning, however, is to dress for temperatures 20 degrees higher than actual ones. Remember, you will work up a sweat.

Two commonly known maxims are that an apple a day keeps the doctor away and that you lose the most heat through your noggin. Though we don't encourage lugging a bushel of apples with you on training runs, we can keep you healthier by suggesting appropriate headwear. For the summer, many athletes prefer baseball style caps. Take our advice and invest in one from a specialty store. They are lightweight and made from a synthetic material that will not result in a sweat-soaked scalp. For the winter, fleece headbands and hats are among the many choices. Select something that is comfortable. And don't forget your face and hands. We swear by neck-warmers and gloves. Although many of these items are manufactured by brand name running lines, you may find inexpensive substitutes to be just as efficient. Once again, experiment.

In addition to keeping a training log and an eye on the weather channel, you will learn the wisdom of layering, as discussed earlier.

in someone else's shoes:

Long distance athletes, in our opinion, are the most idiosyncratic creatures around. They obsess over weather conditions, they have favorite brands of water (yes, water), they perform unusual shoe-lacing rituals and they become very attached to specific pieces of clothing...

Favorite cold weather outfit:
➤   *"LAYERS! Being from Minnesota, the weather can change instantly...you must be prepared for the worst. Long johns, wind pants, long sleeve, outer shell, hat, neck warmer, face warmer...anything you can take off if you get too hot."*
–Amy Bruno, age 29

Favorite warm weather outfit:
➤   *"A sleeveless top with a built-in sports bra, my $14 shorts from Target, Kleenex in my pocket, Thorlos socks and a headband (always)."*
–Brenda Anderson, age 48

Favorite race day outfit:
➤   *"A long pair of Spandex pants (if cold) or Nike shorts with side pockets (if warm), sports bra, and Wright socks (my favorite). I usually start my training in one pair of shoes, then a month or so before the marathon, I start breaking in another pair (same brand and style). I always write my name on my tank top or racing singlet (so people will cheer for me). If it is cold, I wear a long sleeved shirt underneath the tank so it won't cover up my name. Lastly, a Ziplock bag containing Advil, Aquaphor, Immodium AD and money. And a disposable jacket or rain coat!*
–Sara Prendeville, age 27

heart rate monitors

One accessory that deserves special attention is the heart rate monitor. This is simply a device used for measuring your heart rate (how fast your heart is beating). It consists of two parts: a band worn around your rib cage to track your pulse and a display screen worn on the upper arm or wrist, much like a watch. As with most gadgets, heart rate monitors come in a wide array of styles. A basic, no-frills model can be purchased for around $50; it does nothing more than display your heart rate. More sophisticated models record distances, pace, calorie expenditure and more; these can cost up to several hundred dollars. Popular brands are Polar, Cardiosport, Reebok, Nike and Times, just to name a few.

What's the importance of a heart rate monitor? The primary need for such a device is to keep you informed of your level of exertion, or how hard you are exercising. First, you need to determine your maximum heart rate (MHR)—the greatest number of times your heart can beat in one minute. An easy way to calculate your MHR is to use the following equation: MHR= 220 minus your age in years. By knowing this, you can then adapt your heart rate level for different kinds of workouts. For example, during your easy workouts (for recovery or maintenance), you should exercise at about 60-70 percent of your maximum heart rate. To exercise in what is referred to as the aerobic zone, you need to exercise at 80 percent of your maximum heart rate. It is in this level that you are burning the most fat and teaching your body to use fat stores as fuel.

We find that an easier way to gauge the intensity of workouts is to use the "talk test." It is simply this. Keep your easy or maintenance sessions at a conversational pace. If you can carry on a conversation during the walk or run, you are not exceeding the suggested 60 percent of your maximum heart rate level. For more difficult sessions, challenge yourself to train hard enough so that you are not able to say two or three words at a time without gasping for air. This assures you that you are in the aerobic zone.

It is up to you. If you are interested in keeping close, accurate track of your heart rate level, see our Resource Guide for additional information on purchasing the right monitor for your needs. However, you can successfully train for a marathon without utilizing one at all; just trust your intuition, follow common sense advice and "listen to your body."

accessorize

There are a plethora of gadgets at the runner's or walker's disposal today, but we are only going to cover the basic, can't-live-without items found in every marathoner's toolbox.

- Tissues
- Sport watch that gives split times (a must if you are employing the Galloway method)

- Lip balm (especially in winter)
- Lubricating stick (to prevent chafing and blistering on areas of the body prone to friction while running)
- Ibuprofen (We once resorted to bartering with a convenience store clerk during a 13 mile run for a travel size pack of pain reliever. He seemed relieved we didn't ask him to open his register drawer!)
- Water bottle (There are several devices on the market for carrying water. However, if you prefer running unencumbered, simply plot courses that lead you past water stops, such as your home or a convenience store.)
- Sunscreen

Jewelry and make-up are optional, because as much as we yearn to be taken as serious athletes, we also know that some of you may only run one marathon in your lifetime and thus have only one finish line photo with which to impress others. So based on the small likelihood that a person is physically capable of looking sexy after completing a 26.2 mile race, you should go for it. In fact, Boonsom Hartman can give you pointers. A mile before she crossed the finish line of the Honolulu Marathon, this 46-year-old homemaker from Oak Forest,

MEMORY JOGGER…

"Never pack sentimental items or good luck charms along for the run. Leave superstition to the Bingo ladies. I once ran 13 miles with my sister-in-law's weighty Breast Cancer Survivor medal clanging around my neck. The only inspiration it provided was a resolute desire to stop dressing like Mr. T."

Illinois, completed her ritual done in 49 other states and Washington, D.C. She stopped to put on her lipstick. So go ahead. Make Boonsom proud.

We cannot end this chapter without mentioning a final topic, which we confess may be painful for some of you to hear. Let's get honest. Fashion is not always about function, and although many die-hard athletes pride themselves on being more sagacious than chic, we find that to be a fallacy. Hence, cyclists would care little about graphic helmets and all swimmers would wear Speedos (that's a scary thought). This brings us to our topic—fanny packs. Under no circumstances can we find justification for wearing one. The idea behind exercising is to look fit and improve our figures, so why add another tier to your waistline with one of those unsightly contraptions? Functionality was certainly the inspiration for their invention, but fanny packs, in our opinion, are a true fashion "don't." If you are standing in line for Space Mountain at Disneyworld, then maybe, just maybe, your fanny-packed self would not draw attention; but if you are in that elite percentage of very cool people completing a marathon, leave it at home, sister. This is one of those items that should be burned.

lacing it up

- Visit a specialty running/walking store to be fitted for shoes.
- When shopping for socks, pants and tops, buy only those made from

synthetic fibers which wick moisture away from your skin.

- Buy a well constructed, comfortable sports bra.

- Dress appropriately for cold weather by layering.

- Record temperatures in your running log along with what you wear.

- Burn your fanny pack.

You will find that your transformation into a bona fide athlete is a gradual one. Anyone can enter a specialty running store and then leave the premises dressed like an elite athlete, but it is the little things that will disclose your new identity to the world. The bottles of Gatorade stored in your pantry. The smelly gym clothes tossed in the backseat of your car. And the fact that your television is usually tuned in to the weather channel. Acquaint yourself gradually with different attire and accessories for your training adventure, and you will eventually learn what works and what doesn't.

one woman's story

Barbara Rivers of Albuquerque describes herself as a wearer of many hats. She played confidently her roles of mother, chauffeur, teacher and musician. What she never rehearsed, however, was the script now before her as competitive triathlete, racing down the Sandia Foothills of New Mexico on a road bike at the young age of 52.

As an elementary music teacher and first violinist for the New Mexico Symphony, Barbara's days have always been punctuated by harmonic scales and arpeggios. But two years ago the rhythm began to change as she faced a shift of seasons in her life. Her oldest child left for college and her youngest received his driver's license. With much more time on her hands, Barbara listened as the music in her life quickly changed from forte to pianissimo.

It is at this point in Barbara's story you might expect a slice of drama, a gripping climax. But as for drum rolls, there were none. Barbara, like many mothers shuffled to the sidelines as their children learn to fly, stepped back and let them try their wings. She also decided to investigate a friend's offer to join her in training for a marathon. In her typical methodical fashion, she bought a book and started reading. Then she started walking, and eventually running. And not unlike her parenting, her training became a slow and soulful mission of patience and passion. Nine months later Barbara completed her first marathon.

Olympic marathon gold medalist Emil Zatopek said, "If you want to win something, run 100 meters. If you want to experience something, run a marathon." Barbara Rivers can attest to such truth, as her marathon experience granted her a whole new lifestyle change. Running the marathon opened many doors and possibilities for her. She lost 55 pounds, found a wonderful coach, bought a bicycle and began to train for her next goal—a series of sprint and

Olympic distance triathlons. Last winter was a bigger challenge—the Mt. Taylor Winter Quadrathlon, an endurance event consisting of biking, running, cross country skiing and snow shoeing. We were afraid to ask what Barbara's next goal might be, but we feel certain she will face many new seasons in her life, each with its own unpredictable gifts.

It's funny. This refined, erudite lady teaching budding violinists the magic of Haydn, confessed, "I never thought I was that kind of person." The kind of person racing fearlessly into a brutal headwind on an 18-speed racing bike. The kind of person "who likes speed," adds Barbara. She probably understands what Margaret Mitchell meant when she said, "Until you've lost your reputation, you never realize what a burden it was."

over the coffee cup

Barbara's first marathon: Rock'n'Roll Marathon in San Diego

Age: 50

Time: 5:17

Q: Had you participated in many sports before you decided to train for a marathon?

A: No, I didn't run, bike or swim (only the side stroke). I could only run a few minutes at a time when I first started training.

Q: What one thing did you do right during your training?

A: I was not concerned with time, just finishing. I also tried to listen to my body.

Q: What one thing did you do wrong?

A: I did not give myself a lot of recovery time during my training. I would advise others not to think they have to make up any days they miss. Focus on quality, not quantity.

Q: Did you hit the wall during the race?

A: At mile 22, I felt heavy and had to stop for a moment. It felt no better stopping than running, so I just made the decision to keep going.

Q: Any advice for first time marathoners?

A: Always train with a purpose.

Q: Any million dollar trade secrets?

A: Good conversation during your long distance runs!

Running Log

	Day 1	Day 2	Day 3	Day 4
Date				
Distance				
Time	Week	6		
Path/Notes				
Date				
Distance				
Time	Week	7		
Path/Notes				
Date				
Distance				
Time	Week	8		
Path/Notes				
Date				
Distance				
Time	Week	9		
Path/Notes				
Date				
Distance				
Time	Week	10		
Path/Notes				

Part 3

body by design

From Alyce's memoirs -

I didn't keep the written journal throughout our training that Wendy did, although the virtual journal I kept is easy to tap back into. It will be forever written in my heart. So many of our runs were memorable, but one in particular comes to mind. It was memorable in its own right—the 20 miler, the longest run we would take prior to accomplishing "the big one." We knew as we met in the pre-dawn hours that morning that it would be a special run, the culmination of several months of training. The marathon itself was a separate entity, distanced from all of the other runs by its sheer magnitude, its status as "the goal." But the 20 miler was the granddaddy of our training runs and we were like little schoolgirls that morning, chatting giddily as we waited for the large training group to assemble, eager to take on this master challenge.

As we headed out, we fell comfortably into our routine, breaking off into our own little groups. We were blessed to have been "adopted" in the early months of training by the most entertaining ensemble of twenty-somethings, who kept us wonderfully distracted with their stories and their laughter. They often argued that we had adopted them and that it was us who did the entertaining. (Come to think of it, the sight of us running probably was good entertainment!) Within our group, as so often happens, there were six distinctive personalities, each of whom added a special flavor. We had a chatterbox, a jokemiester, a caretaker, a sentimentalist, a quiet one and a pack leader who kept us from losing pace as we immersed ourselves in conversation. And yet despite—or perhaps because of—our diversity, our bunch had a unique flavor all its own. We always seemed to draw attention and on several occasions would find other groups or individuals latching on to share in our fun.

And so it was no surprise that day at mile eight when a 40-something-year-old man of athletic build started running beside us. My training partners would have you believe that I was the one responsible; they always accused me of picking up "strays." I happen to believe it was divine intervention. He was tall, lean and muscular with a ready smile and was appropriately attired in Nike garb, by appearances an obvious athlete. I was frankly quite flattered that he chose to run alongside us. The only puzzling feature was a pair of pressed pants he draped over his arm as he ran. He was quite engaging and I found myself moving ahead of the others to keep pace with and listen to his conversation. Yet I was keenly aware of the whispers and giggles emanating from my comrades as they maintained a slower stride behind us. On occasion I would glance over my shoulder and catch them trying furtively to motion me back to the safety of the group. At mile 10, we stopped at a water break station to refuel and watched with curiosity as he guzzled two cups of Gatorade and hungrily wiped out a bowlful of animal crackers, but it was his question "How far are you going?" that finally opened our eyes. Our newfound and mysterious running mate wasn't a member of any training team after all. He just liked to run. I was certain when I told him that we had 10 miles yet to go, he would turn and head back to where he had first joined us. Instead, he was clearly excited that we had a lot of road yet to cover and was more than happy to go wherever that road happened to take us.

In the miles that lay ahead of us, the initial reservations of my friends melted away as we listened to and grew attached to this simple man. He introduced himself as Curtis. Simply Curtis. No last name, no car, no steady job and no family. The pants he carried were his "church pants." He had just picked them up from the cleaners and seemed to have forgotten they were still in his arms. He lived alone in a small apartment with little to show for his years. Yet it was clearly apparent that he had his faith and he had his legs and the two kept him moving through life quite well.

He listened, he laughed, he shared, he even led us in a few soulful tunes...and he ran, with seemingly little effort, with the grace of a youthful athlete and with obvious joy in the company of those around him.

Yes, he was different, or so society would label him. On another day, had I been alone, I may not have been comfortable in his presence. But this was a different day, a day when perhaps my eyes and my heart were more open than ever before and by mile 18, Curtis had become a full-fledged member of our group.

We turned a few heads as we made it down the home stretch that day, six slow white women led by one towering black male, head thrown back, leading us in song, with a smile that stretched from ear to ear across his face—no different than the smiles painted on ours. Curtis (or Curtis Gump as we now affectionately refer to him) brought us home that day, shouting words of encouragement in the last quarter-mile and high-fiving us as we came to the finish.

Looking back, I feel certain we had an angel in our midst that day, wonderfully symbolic of all the gifts that had been given us during the course of our months of training. Curtis embodied those gifts. He was a reminder to keep our hearts open, to reach out and to embrace the unexpected surprises and opportunities that come our way. A reminder to never let fear prevent us from growing, learning and exploring all that life has to offer. A gentle reminder to embrace our differences and to appreciate the richness that diversity adds to our lives. A gentle reminder to keep on smiling.

We never saw Curtis again after that day. I don't know if he ever got a job, or a car or a house. I don't know if he was ever blessed with a family. But in the brief time I was able to spend getting to know him, I do feel certain of one thing—Curtis is still running. And so am I.

chapter 7

no need for pedicures: injury prevention

Before December of 2003, we both were typical mothers, wives and civic-minded individuals. We held jobs, we drove carpools and we worked hair highlights and occasional manicures into our schedules with enviable efficiency. Our days were comprised of much of the same things as yours. Then we set a common goal to train for a marathon. We still chauffeured carpools and we still sorted laundry, but at the end of the day we went to sleep with a secret tucked under our pillows. We were marathoners.

As our training progressed, fatigue did creep into our lives, some days more than others. When you take your body from zero to 80 in a matter of months, aches and pains are bound to surface. Walk into the home of any marathoner-in-training and I bet you will find pain relieving ointment on her nightstand and cold packs in her freezer. It was no different for us. We nursed tender muscles and wrapped sore ankles, all the time questioning our sanity. With a few roadblocks along the way, we managed to stay true to our schedule.

When May arrived, amazingly we had run over 300 miles together. We endured nasty spills on loose gravel, slips on unforseen patches of ice, tears of pain and fears of betrayal by these middle-aged bodies. And with encouragement, a belief in ourselves, and more than an inkling of common sense, we made it to the starting line. We were still wives, we were still mothers, but when we stole glimpses of ourselves when walking past a mirror, we were standing just a bit taller. We were marathoners.

Throughout training, you may find yourself faced with a number of obstacles, one being injury. Take heart. We will provide you with preventative actions to implement, treatments to mend the body and tonics to nourish the soul.

ounce of prevention

We won't be so cliché as to assert that an ounce of prevention is worth a, well, you know the rest. But we will stress the vital importance of preventative care when training for a marathon. If you are in your twenties and feeling invincible, you may not feel compelled to pay strict attention to our counsel, but this advice applies to all ages. We listened to the experts when we embarked on our adventure (we were too afraid not to) and we stayed relatively injury free. In addition to the experts, and perhaps more importantly, we LISTENED TO OUR BODIES. You may have heard the saying, "It is easy to train hard; it is hard to train smart." In some perverse way, pushing through a 14 mile run on a twisted ankle seems more heroic than giving yourself a week of rest. Heroic, maybe, but not wise. One week off now more often than not helps you to avoid three or four weeks off later. Your body's words are throbs and twinges. Heed their message and rest.

In researching ways to prevent and treat injuries during marathon training, we consulted with Daniel R. Brauning, MPT, ATC, of Oxford Physical Therapy Centers, Cincinnati based facilities which specialize in sports medicine. He shared with us that out of the hundreds of runners he sees each year, the majority are women. "I would say that 65 to 70 percent are women. As a general rule, injuries also increase with age." Brauning adds that "training for a marathon can be a wonderfully healthy experience for body and mind if you do it the correct way." So heed our no nonsense advice and stay injury free throughout your marathon experience.

Shoe selection. Get fitted by a professional with the correct pair of shoes right away! It is common knowledge in the running/walking community that when foot and ankle problems surface, it is likely time for a new pair of sneakers. Now is not the time to bargain shop. Invest in a quality pair from a specialized running/walking store. Likewise, if the shoes you're currently donning cost more than all your Easter outfits (for the last three years), don't rule them out as the possible culprit of a recent ache or pain. As your training progresses and you grow stronger, your biomechanics change and so do your physical needs. When a problem arises, check out your shoes. And it bears repeating—seek the advice of an expert! Hopefully, if you stumble upon this dictate often enough during the course of reading this book, you may avoid stumbling into problems along the way.

Stretching. Warming your muscles up by stretching them out before a run is recommended (a warm shower works also). Five to ten minutes of gentle stretching or jogging in place increases blood flow and oxygen to the muscles and improves the range of motion at the joints. However, according to Daniel R. Brauning, certified physical therapist and athletic trainer, the best time for stretching is after a warm up and immediately after a run. This keeps you flexible, reduces the risk of muscle soreness and helps prevent injury. "Many of the most common running injuries are caused by poor flexibility in specific muscles groups," Brauning explains.

Think of stretching as part of your walk or run, not as an "extra" if time permits. Try also not to overcomplicate the routine; just memorize a few simple tips. Start with the feet and work upward, stretching basic muscle groups. Hold each stretch for 30 seconds to one minute, and do not stretch with pain. Brauning also provided us with this fundamental list of stretches to perform after each run.

Gastroc/soleus stretch (calves)

Stand facing a wall with right foot about six inches away from wall, knee slightly bent. Place left foot about 18 inches away from wall. While keeping left heel on the floor, lean from hips into the wall. Hold for at least 30 seconds; repeat with opposite leg.

Stand facing a wall, assuming the same position as above. Bend both knees, then lean into the wall. Hold for at least 30 seconds; repeat with opposite leg.

Piriformis stretch

Sit up straight in a chair; cross one leg over (as shown); lean forward. Hold for 30 seconds; repeat with opposite leg.

Quadriceps stretch

Stand on right foot; lift left foot up close behind the buttocks. Grab left foot with left hand and gently pull it back and up. Hold for 30 seconds; repeat with opposite leg.

Hamstring stretch

While lying on back, raise one leg (try to keep it straight). Grab the raised leg and gently pull it towards you. Hold for 30 seconds; repeat with opposite leg.

Abductor stretch (inner thighs)

While sitting on the ground, place bottoms of feet against each other. Gently push knees downward with elbows. Hold for 30 seconds.

Hip flexor stretch

Kneel on left knee, left foot straight behind. Place right foot on floor, bending right knee at 90 degree angle. With hands at waist, lean body forward, keeping back in line with hips. Hold for 30 seconds; repeat with opposite leg.

Lower back stretch

While lying on back, left leg straight, lift right knee up and pull in towards chest. Hold for 30 seconds; repeat with opposite leg. Then lift both knees up and pull in towards chest. Hold for 30 seconds.

Ice. You probably won't find this recommendation mentioned in any other manual as an orthodox prevention to injury, but we're not at all convinced that running 26.2 miles is orthodox behavior. Nurse sore ankles and knees with 10-15 minutes of icing when you return home from a walk or run. Sounds silly, but we've tried this and it works. We spoke with physical therapist Daniel Brauning and he confirmed our recommendation. "Ice has very powerful physiological effects," he explains, "It produces strong analgesia, reduces metabolic activity, slows nerve conduction and decreases muscle tone and spasticity. ..I highly recommend that you use ice after runs ...it is a great preventative medicine."

Strength training. It is often difficult enough to include four runs or walks into your weekly schedule; adding occasional dumb-bell routines is even harder. However, if you are worried about a potential problem (weak knees, for example), strength training for that particular body part helps toughen weak muscles and prevent future injuries.

World class runner and marathon coach Karen Cosgrove extols the benefits of resistance training so emphatically that she even suggests replacing one of your easy training walks/runs during the week with a weight lifting session, if a hectic agenda necessitates a sacrifice. "The benefits of a balanced program far outweigh the conditioning lost from one missed walk or run," she explains.

No need for pedicures. We weren't joking. Save the pedicure for after the marathon. Those calluses actually offer built-in protection, which you will need as you discover the toll training exacts on your feet. You will likely encounter a black toenail or two as well. Consider such battle wounds your badge of courage. Keep toenails cut short and leave the calluses alone; there will be time enough later to pamper the feet that are about to take you on the journey of a lifetime.

common injuries

Despite your best efforts at prevention, you may find yourself suffering from an injury. Without becoming overly technical, we want to alert you to some of the most common injuries experienced by avid walkers and runners.

Plantar fasciitis. We like to keep things simple. If your heel screams with pain the minute you first place your foot on the floor in the morning, then you are most likely suffering from plantar fasciitis. A band of tissue called the

MEMORY JOGGER...
"Stock your fridge with lots of cold packs to try to avoid using frozen foods as substitutes. After my first marathon, I blindly grabbed a package of frozen rolls from the freezer. I sank into bed, grateful for a chance to relax and ice my sore knees. I awoke the next morning weighted under a mammoth mound of risen dough, befitting of an 'I Love Lucy' episode."

plantar fascia runs from the heel to the base of the toes. If it is torn or inflamed, pain in the heel results. The discomfort is known to lessen as you walk and "work it out," but don't be fooled into thinking this problem will cease on its own. It will not. Take a break from running and rest for a while, stretch the calf muscles regularly, apply ice to the arch of the foot and see a professional if the pain persists. He will probably fit you with orthotic insoles, many of which are relatively inexpensive and sold at specialty running stores, as under and overpronation and improper footwear are common culprits.

A tidbit to speed recovery is to keep your running shoes by the side of your bed. Before stepping onto the floor barefoot upon awakening, slip into your shoes and enjoy that first cup of coffee looking like the true athlete you are becoming. This prevents you from stretching out the fascia band too quickly after a night of inactivity.

Shin splints. If you experience pain at the front of your lower leg along the shin, you may become suspicious of medial tibial stress syndrome, more commonly known as shin splints. The best course of action here is to rest. The sooner you rest, the sooner it will heal. Stretching the calf muscles regularly, applying ice and switching from pavement to softer trails also helps. If pain persists, you may want to see a professional to analyze your running style and check your footwear.

Iliotibial band syndrome. Another technical term to be incorporated into your repertoire of runners' lingo is iliotibial band, or IT band for short. The IT band is a band of tissue that runs down the outside of your thigh from your hip past your knee joint. If tight or inflamed, it begins to rub on the bone at the knee, causing pain. People generally complain of a sharp or burning sensation at the lateral aspect of the knee. It may begin as a dull ache but could become quite severe if not treated with rest. Overpronation and weak hip muscles are contributing factors. However, routine stretching of the IT band, quadriceps and hamstrings can help. There are also elastic IT straps or braces that can be worn while running to help absorb shock.

Runner's knee. Don't even worry with pronouncing its technical name, *chondromalacia patellae*. It is simply a gradual pain that occurs under your kneecap and worsens with continued activity. The cartilage wears away or becomes inflamed, usually from overuse, and requires rest. It is often accompanied by swelling. Applying ice to the knees, strengthening the quadriceps, regular stretching and proper footwear help.

Achilles tendonitis. This is the inflammation of the tendon which attaches the two major calf muscles to the heel bone. During training, this tendon can receive tensile forces over eight times your body weight. This can eventually cause the tendon to fatigue and break down. Stretching, correct footwear and being careful not to overtrain can help.

Stress fractures. These are simply small fractures in the bone. Activity related pain gradually worsens if not given rest. Increasing mileage too quickly and overtraining are contributing factors. Daniel Brauning, Cincinnati based physical therapist, says that he often sees stress fractures afflicting women involved in accelerated training programs. "You do not need to run six days a week to train for a race," he states frankly, "Another misconception is that you have to build your long runs over 20 miles…20 miles is enough, doing 22 and 24 mile runs is too hard on the body and will cause injury or fatigue you too much. Leave the 26.2 mile run for race day! More is not better."

Tendonitis and Bursitis. If you experience any swelling or tenderness in your ankles, feet or knees, the diagnosis could possibly be tendonitis or bursitis. These are general terms describing irritation and inflammation of a

> MEMORY JOGGER…"An ingenious friend picked up a one inch diameter stick along the course one day and used it as a rolling pin to massage the length of my outer leg (IT band) which was screaming with pain. Miraculously, the pain subsided (for at least a few more miles). My dependency on the stick grew to mimic Tom Hanks's attachment to the volleyball in 'Shipwrecked,' so it wasn't long before my running mates nicknamed it Wilson. Somewhere along the line we painted a face on him and our unlikely running mascot joined us for every run thereafter!"

tendon or a bursa (sacs between moving structures such as bones and muscles). The most common cause of tendonitis or bursitis is overuse. These should be seen as warning signs. Temporarily stop your activity and give your body a rest. If not, a more severe problem, such as stress fractures, may result.

We know that when watching your training companions dart past your house from the confines of your living room sofa, a week of rest will seem like a month. Don't despair; your body needs it. It is when you fail to listen to your body that you face the possibility of missing race day.

Black toenails. By now you have probably learned that marathon training is not an entirely glamorous undertaking. This malady known as black toenails proves it. You may actually find one of your toenails turning black due to a blood blister developing underneath the nail bed. Because women generally carry their weight differently than men, they tend to have wider feet. During a long distance walk or run, constant friction or ill fitting shoes may lead to blisters and, yes, a black toenail or two. Keeping your nails cut short, applying Vaseline or another lubricant to your feet before the run and wearing properly fitted shoes help.

a word of warning

Exercise common sense when treating minor aches and pains. Reaching for the bottle of aspirin should not become routine. Some over-the-counter pain relievers are helpful for treating minor problems but should not be used to mask more serious pain. Also, current research suggests that too frequent dependency on nonsteroidal aids, such as ibuprofen and naproxen, can be harmful. Adopt a common sense approach when it comes to injuries and always LISTEN TO YOUR BODY.

recovery

It is very likely you will complete your marathon training with no injuries at all, especially if you "train smart, not hard," as we mentioned previously. Helping your body to recover from those long distance training sessions is also essential.

Rest. Key to recovery is adequate rest. Overtraining is the top reason marathon hopefuls fail to cross the finish line, or rather the starting line. Rest days are built into the schedule as provisions for your muscles to recover. In fact, listening to your body means heeding all its messages, not just the aches and pains. If you are simply tired and feeling run-down, it may be wiser to forego one of your easy walks/runs than to push yourself too hard.

Protein. In addition, many athletes claim that consuming protein, such as a protein shake or drink, immediately after a long run helps promote tissue healing.

Massage. We have found this to be one of the most effective ways to speed recovery after a long distance run or walk. If you have never experienced a post workout massage, you may believe the fatigue and soreness after a 16 or 18 mile training session is untreatable; but if you have indulged in a sports massage after a long distance jaunt, you will become a firm believer in its magic. It helps to flush the build-up of lactic acid and waste products out of muscles, and an experienced massage therapist can often identify and work out trouble spots long before they develop into injuries. Once your runs reach 15 miles and over, treat yourself to an occasional sports massage.

lacing it up

- Remember to LISTEN TO YOUR BODY.
- Get fitted by a professional for the correct pair of shoes.
- Routinely stretch after every walk or run.
- Ice sore muscles.
- Strength train for weak knees and body parts.
- Save the pedicure for after the marathon!
- Seek help from a professional sports therapist for any persistent injury.
- Speed muscle and tissue recovery with proper rest, protein replenishment and massage therapy.

one woman's story

According to Carrie, her mother Katie often speaks of all the different shoes she has worn in her life. It should come as no surprise, then, that a pair of sneakers would be one of them. Katie Berg, also in the words of her daughter, is "the woman who never stops." With a successful career as a nurse, Katie acknowledges that she is part of the "sandwich generation," as much of her energy has been divided between rearing children and tending to aging parents.

In July of 2003, however, Katie's contagious energy began to dwindle. Both her professional life and personal one were in the throws of change. The hospital at which she worked was undergoing a transition, and her daughter was planning an upcoming wedding. Katie attributed her recent tiredness to the stresses of life.

Three months later, Katie treated herself to a Disney World vacation for her fiftieth birthday, but even this retreat proved no sanctuary from her increasing fatigue. She soon found herself in a doctor's office. After a series of tests (and then more tests) she was told she needed to see an oncologist. Before New Year's Day, she underwent surgery, and in January she began chemotherapy. Katie received injections each Thursday and returned to work each Monday. It was not until February that she was forced to surrender to the rigors of treatment and take a leave of absence from her job. The woman who was described as "typically spirited" by her friends and co-workers found herself lying on her couch for months.

The cycles of Katie's saga seemed to fluctuate with the seasons. Last fall, as trees dropped their brilliant leaves, Katie's health spiraled downward. When snow storms drifted in, the news of Katie's cancer punctuated her holidays. And as spring growth began to bud anew on the old lilac bush in her yard, Katie also awakened with new conviction. She decided to go on a bike ride.

Life picked up its pace for Katie, and one evening she accompanied her daughter, at Carrie's insistence, to an informational meeting about marathon training with the Leukemia and Lymphoma Society. Little did Carrie know that her mother would be the first one in the room to sign up! Katie didn't sign up to walk the half-marathon; she didn't sign up to run the half-marathon. Katie, still weak from her bout with cancer, signed on the dotted line to RUN THE FULL MARATHON.

Carrie recalls their first day of training. The schedule stipulated two miles. She went to bed early, drank plenty of water and met her mother the next morning for their two mile trek--which they did…in 45 minutes! That is how training started--with Katie monitoring her breathing, Carrie monitoring her mom and both of them counting their blessings. With hot coffee and a bucket full of gear, Katie greeted her daughter every Saturday morning just as the sun began to rise, and off to the park they would go. As Carrie's pace quickened, they often separated during training sessions. However, Carrie remembers running beside her mother during Katie's first solid mile as being a "glorious day." "The fun thing about my mom's training was that she was excited about all of the 'little' things. Things some runners take for granted were huge for my mom." Katie's first official blister became her battle wound. She was the first on the trail to give each passing team member a high five. And every time her daughter whisked by her, she never failed to mouth the words, "I love you."

Adopted by her Team in Training comrades, Katie became everyone's inspiration. Although her pace was slow, her teammates would nonetheless wait for her at the finish line each week, proud of her determination. Then, at the crescendo of her training, Katie experienced an injury, severe tendonitis and a nagging IT band. She was uncertain if she would be able to complete the full race and contemplated running only half. She examined where she was one year earlier (about to fall victim to an undiscriminating disease) and where she was at that moment (alive). Carrie never saw her mother cry once during her battle with cancer. She saw her mom cry during marathon training. That night. The night this remarkable, spirited woman decided that anything less than 26.2 miles would be a compromise. After all, she was alive.

Somewhere planted in Katie Berg's heart was the notion that since 2003 had begun on a note of grief, 2005 must debut with celebration. Visits to a chiropractor and a new pair of shoes helped heal her injury, but nothing could assuage her fear. Nonetheless, she packed her bag and once again traveled to the fantasy oasis of Disney World, this time to run the Walt Disney Marathon, all 26.2 miles of it.

Race day arrived, dressed in Disney fashion hubbub and 83 degree heat. Carrie quickly found her pace and soon surpassed one of her loyal training buddies. With each mile, she kept wondering, "How is my mom?" At the finish line, she hydrated then instantly turned her focus onto finding her mother. She was able to enter Katie's bib number into her brother's cell phone (isn't technology amazing?) and track her progress. At each checkpoint, a text message appeared. Katie had not been spotted since the half-way point. Had she been injured? Tried to push herself too far, too fast? Then a message appeared on the screen; Katie had passed mile 20. Those next six miles, Carrie recalls, were the longest moments of her life. She sat with her husband, brother and stepfather… and waited. She reflected on the past year and, through her sweat and tears, prayed.

Her mother's recollection of those last six miles is quite different. Just as she had done with cancer, she confronted and conquered the weariness taking over her body and mind. She began to get involved outside of herself, engaging with those around her. As she trod through the theme park, she shouted to curious onlookers, "I need some of your MAGIC!" She held out her hand in high five style to the crowds behind the roped barriers. It WORKED! Smiles and cheers showered Katie, as some folks even ran to form a line ahead of her just to offer the crazed and exhilarated woman a high five to magically boost her along her way. As Katie recalls, a few of her running comrades fell behind as they probably thought she was truly nuts, but it didn't matter. Katie knew that those connections she made with humanity, if only for fleeting moments, gave her life, energy and spirit. And she started thinking about her team and the purpose for which she was running. She started thinking about her friend's mother who didn't have a chance to beat the cancer that took her life 40 years ago, her coach who had lost her own mother to leukemia when she was only five, and her own family—especially her daughter—and how her illness had impacted them. All of a sudden she knew she was going to finish the race…because of those little girls who grew up without their mothers…so she could celebrate her daughter who grew up with hers.

As far as Kodak moments go, Katie's finish line performance was certainly one. Arms raised, running and smiling. Katie's husband and children, screaming and shouting, nearly tackled her with hugs. This lady had fought and won yet another battle. She had once told her daughter that she always looked at marathon runners in awe and admired their courage. Now she is the person others will behold in awe. She is the marathoner, whose journey covered more ground than a route through Disney World.

The celebration did not stop at the finish line. Upon returning home, Katie's former high school classmates surprised her with a trophy and cake. Her Bridge group congratulated her with a dozen red roses. But perhaps the greatest gift Katie received was proving to the world and to herself that life is worth fighting for. Lance Armstrong authored the phrase, "I take nothing for granted. I now have only good days, or great days." Katie Berg lives it.

over the coffee cup

Katie and Carrie's first marathon: Disney Marathon

Carrie:

Age: 27

Time: 5:02

Q: What was your impetus for tackling a marathon?

A: I wanted to challenge myself to the fullest and share an extraordinary moment with my family. I was not the first to sign up however. Once my mom said she would do it…I HAD to!

Q: Any fundraising tips to share?

A: Fundraising was remarkably easier than many people think. We had a Halloween Party and everyone donated money to the charity.

Q: Did you ever hit the wall?

A: At mile 24 when I caught a whiff of the funnel cake stand at Epcot Center, I thought I was going to hurl. But other than that, no.

Q: What was one thing you did right during your training?

A: I celebrated every victory, big or small.

Q: What was one thing you did wrong?

A: I cursed a lot towards the end.

Q: Any advice for first-time marathoners?

A: Have fun. Don't worry about your time. Smile the whole time and enjoy the moment.

Q: Any million dollar trade secrets?

A: BodyGlide everywhere! In between your toes, your bra, inside your shorts. BodyGlide is not for the weak—it is for everyone.

Q: What life lessons did you learn from running a marathon?

A: The whole time I smiled. I smiled because I had pushed my body and spirit to a new level. I smiled because although there was pain, I knew that I wanted to do this again. I smiled because a marathon should be the way all people live their lives. During the race there are a lot of people on the sidelines yelling your name and encouraging you. Can you imagine if everything in life was that way? As a society we should be cheering on our family, friends and strangers every day to do better.

Katie:

Age: 51

Time: "I finished." (6:58 to be exact.)

Q: What was your impetus for tackling a marathon?

A: I always wanted to! I have always done what was before me...because I HAD to. If someone had asked me "What do YOU want to do?" I would have been speechless. I had never thought about it. My motto was "you will because you have to." This marathon, however, was all because I WANTED to. It was also my way of showing cancer who was boss!

Q: How did you hold up during training?

A: Some days good, some days not. I'm not the fastest runner. I would jog for two minutes, then walk for five, until I worked up to running a full mile without a walk break.

Q: Any fundraising tips?

A: My fundraising was solely from a letter-writing campaign. Also, my friends were emotionally and financially supportive. One of my closest high school friends had lost her mother to leukemia when my classmate was only nine. I knew that this loss was the most significant event that shaped her life, so I asked if I could run and fundraise in her mother's memory. I sent out letters to all our high school classmates, and the response was overwhelming.

Q: What one thing did you do right during your training or the race?

A: During the marathon, strike up conversations and learn more about the people who are along the way. I met a very inspirational woman during the race and stayed with this positive person for a while just to soak up her story. Before we knew it, five miles had passed.

Q: What one thing did you do wrong?

A: I wish I had incorporated more weight training for overall body conditioning.

Q: Did you ever hit the wall?

A: Not really. What happened to me from mile 20 to 26 was a mental process. I did, however, pay very close attention to my pace in relation to my heart rate. I wore one of the Polar pulse monitors so as to know what was going on. (Of all the pieces of training gear, I have to say that the pulse monitor was the most beneficial for my state of fitness and ability.)

Q: Any million dollar trade secrets?

A: I truly believe that the "million dollar secret" is different for each of us and has to come from within. It may be worth a million only to the one who discovers it. I wouldn't trade or sell mine for a million…what I gained is worth more.

chapter 8

sole food: nutrition

"One cannot think well, love well, sleep well, if one has not dined well."
- Virginia Wolff

We couldn't have said it better! We can only assume that had Virginia Wolff been in training for a marathon, she would have added "run well" to her infamous saying. We will also presume that dear Virginia knew that dining well spoke less about the volume of food upon the table than the quality of the victuals. In today's fast-paced world, busy women often make food choices that are more convenient than nutritional. We are also easily lured by the promises of cleverly marketed fad diets and the confusing assortment of health foods from which to choose. The product labels are enough to challenge anyone short of a dietician. Reduced fat, no fat, low fat, sugar free, fat free, baked, whole-grain, multi-grain, light, dark, polyunsaturated?! At times the array of products that lines our grocer's shelf can be overwhelming, the selection so vast and the nutrition labels so detailed it is dizzying. One can't help but appreciate the simplistic wisdom shared by comedian Buddy Hackett who once said, "My mother's menu consisted of two choices: Take it or leave it!" By the same token, choice is good if we know enough to make wise ones.

By virtue of the fact that you are reading this book we already know you can make good choices. (Unless, of course, this is on the required reading list for a self-improvement class you are taking, in which case it is your professor who makes good selections!) If you have made it to this chapter, we will also assume that you have already made the decision to train for a marathon. Speaking from personal experience, nutritional considerations were not at the forefront of our initial foray into the world of running. Personal goals and inspiration were what drew us into this amazing endeavor, but it wasn't too far into our journey that we realized the impact our nutritional choices would have on the outcome. Our bodies are amazing vehicles, astonishingly willing to go wherever our hearts and minds will them to go…to a point. Training for an ultra-endurance sport such as a marathon quickly defines that point. It is then that wise nutritional choices will be rewarded with the best performance your body is capable of giving.

It is important to understand that women have different nutritional requirements than men. Perhaps more importantly, woman athletes have greater nutritional requirements than their sedentary counterparts. According to Dr. Walter R. Frontera, M.D. and Richard P. Adams, Ph.D., "During sustained exercise such as marathon running, total body energy requirements increase 10 to 20 times above resting values." Before we discuss those specific requirements, it is important that we understand the six basic components of nutrition and what they will bring to the training table.

carbohydrates

"If you ate pasta and antipasta every day, would you still be hungry?"

–George Carlin

Sorry, Dr. Atkins, but we endurance athletes love our carbohydrates! They are our bodies' greatest source of energy. Carbohydrates are converted by the body into glucose, which can be used immediately for energy or stored in the muscles as glycogen. These precious stores of glycogen act as high-octane fuel and are used by athletes to power their muscles for maximum performance during long distance runs. If you ever "hit the wall" during a run, chances are you've run out of carbohydrates.

Simple carbohydrates. Keep in mind as well that not all carbs are created equal. Remember those "empty calories" our mothers used to warn us about?

They were probably referring to simple carbohydrates, which are the most basic form of sugar, such as candy, sweets and sodas. Need a quick burst of energy? Simple carbohydrates are the answer. (Gummy bears were a welcomed snack we relied on during our weekly long runs!) Just keep in mind that the energy burst they deliver is short-lived, so limit your intake of these "Simple Simons." They should comprise less than 10 percent of your diet.

Complex carbohydrates. If you are looking for a long-term relationship, complex carbohydrates are your best bet. Because they provide energy on a more consistent basis, they are considered fuel-efficient. Foods that are rich in complex carbohydrates include fruits, vegetables, pasta, beans, bread, potatoes and rice. Dr. Liz Applegate, author of *Eat Smart, Play Hard* and nutrition columnist for Runner's World magazine, recommends that 50 percent of total calories for a runner's diet be comprised of complex carbohydrates. "Aim for 400 carbohydrate grams (1,600 calories) as a daily goal—more if you do high mileage or if you eat considerably more than 2,500 total calories a day." Keep in mind that we do have a limited ability to store carbs and it is therefore recommended that we spread our carbohydrate intake out over several meals/snacks throughout the day. Variety is also key when it comes to carbohydrates, as they provide many nutrients that are important for our overall health. Dr. Applegate adds, "If you don't come close to the recommended amount of carbohydrates and you exercise for an hour or more at a time, consider drinking a carbohydrate-loaded sports drink before or after your workouts."

fats

"There is no sincerer love than the love of food."

–George Bernard Shaw

In today's world of low fat, reduced fat and fat free foods, one might begin to presume that fats are the bad guys. Let us put that myth to rest. Our bodies need fats to keep us warm, protect our organs, absorb and move nutrients around and to also aid in hormone production. As with carbohydrates, it is important to understand the different types of fats and which ones better serve our sports nutrition needs.

Saturated fats and trans fat. These fats are probably what have given fats their bad reputation. The American Heart Association recommends that we limit these fats to less than 10 percent of our total caloric intake. Trans fat, the ultimate "bad guy," raises LDL (bad cholesterol) and lowers HDL (good cholesterol). It is found in vegetable shortening, many fast foods and some margarines. Saturated fat raises both HDL and LDL, so it isn't quite the bad guy that trans fat is. Saturated fat can be found in red meat, chocolate and dairy products such as cheese, milk and ice cream.

Poly-unsaturated fat. This category of fats is a step above the saturated and trans fats. Polyunsaturated fat lowers LDL (bad cholesterol) and raises HDL (good cholesterol). It can be found in some vegetable oils, including corn, soybean and safflower. The illustrious Omega-3 fats (found in some fish and flaxseed oil) are also polyunsaturated and have been credited with decreasing the risk of heart disease and arthritis.

Mono-unsaturated fat. The "good guys" in the fat family, mono-unsaturated fats are responsible for lowering LDL levels and raising HDL levels and have also been credited with reducing the risk of several kinds of cancer as well as heart disease. These fats include olives, olive oil, avocados and nuts. This is the family of fats that will best meet your sports nutrition needs and should comprise the majority of the 25-30 percent of your daily calories from fats.

proteins

"Let the stoics say what they please, we do not eat for the good of living, but because the meat is savory and the appetite is keen."

–Ralph Waldo Emerson

Proteins are the essential part of your diet for building muscles and tendons, repairing tissue and regulating hormones. (We can all appreciate the importance of hormone regulation!) They are also vital in transporting carbohydrates throughout our bodies, a necessity for endurance athletes. Because of their efficiency in helping move carbohydrates more quickly into the muscles, proteins have earned a respected place at the post-run training table. More recent research debates the endurance-enhancing role protein can play when consumed during your runs. Evidence of this is apparent in the carbohydrate-protein sports drinks now on the market. Understandably, a deficiency of protein will cause fatigue and slow recovery during and after workouts. For maximum performance, protein should account for 15-20 percent of your total caloric intake. According to Runner's World nutrition editor Dr. Liz Applegate, "Sedentary people need 50-70 grams of protein a day to keep them going. Fit people need about 70-100 grams daily to take care of muscle repair and increased energy requirements." Low-fat or fat-free dairy products as well as lean meat, fish and soy products are excellent sources of protein for the long-distance athlete.

vitamins and minerals

"Let food be your medicine and medicine be your food."

–Hippocrates

A well-balanced diet that includes a variety of fruits, vegetables, lean meats and non-processed foods in the ratios mentioned above should ensure that you are meeting all of your sports nutrition requirements. Yet, even the best intentioned of us may find it hard to measure up to the increased nutritional demands that marathon training places on the body. Although your body is more efficient at absorbing the nutrients found in whole food than it is with those found in vitamin supplements, it is still our recommendation that you take a multivitamin with mineral supplement each day. If nothing else, it may give you a little peace of mind, and we could all use an ample supply of that.

Some vitamins worth mentioning in terms of their importance to the female athlete include vitamin C, vitamin E, and vitamins B1 and B2.

Vitamin C is an essential antioxidant that is used to make collagen, an important protein used in the structure of connective tissue and bones. It also helps to boost the immune system. A deficiency of this vitamin can negatively impact physical performance. Active women need 75 milligrams of vitamin C each day, which can be obtained through citrus fruits, berries, tomatoes and dark green leafy vegetables.

Vitamin E aids in the protection of tissues against damage as well as promotes normal growth and development. Although not as easily obtainable through the diet, it can be found in nuts, cereals, wheat germ and dark green leafy vegetables.

Vitamins B1 and B2 both assist in the release of energy, B1 (Thiamine) from carbohydrates and B2 (Riboflavin) from fats and protein. Understandably, endurance athletes benefit from adequate amounts of these two vitamins in their diets in order to fuel their muscles. B1 is found in whole grain cereals, beans, peas and pork, while B2 can be obtained through dairy products, eggs, breads, liver and green vegetables.

Zinc and iron. Additionally, Dr. Liz Applegate, renowned nutrition expert and faculty member of the nutrition department at UC-Davis, states that runners often skimp on zinc and iron, two trace minerals found predominantly in red meat. Iron is especially important for menstruating women because of its role in red cell formation. Studies have shown that more than half of all women runners are iron deficient. Low iron levels result in fatigue and poor endurance. Zinc is involved in the metabolism of carbohydrates, proteins and fats. "Though research hasn't linked zinc and iron deficiency with increased injury rates, I've noticed the connection when working with injured athletes and so have many of my sports-nutrition colleagues." Dr. Applegate recommends 15 milligrams of zinc and 18 milligrams of iron each day. "Most runners don't consume near that much, which is why I recommend eating a zinc and iron fortified breakfast cereal or taking a multivitamin that contains both minerals."

Calcium helps to preserve bone density and is essential to the diet of an endurance athlete. Although athletes in general have stronger bones than normal sedentary adults, it is strongly recommended that female athletes consume between 1,000-1,500 mg of calcium per day. Good sources of calcium include dairy products, dark green leafy vegetables (once again!) and fortified juices and cereals.

Magnesium helps to build bones and muscles. It is important for endurance athletes because of its role in energy production and its involvement in nerve and muscle functions. It can be found in whole grains, nuts and (you guessed it) dark green leafy vegetables.

water and sports drinks

"Water is the only drink for a wise man."

–Henry David Thoreau

Yes, you're still in the nutrition chapter…where better to include the body's most important nutrient and the one so essential to an athlete's performance? An endurance athlete's body is comprised of about 60 percent water, nearly the same percentage as that which makes up the earth! During aerobic exercise, our muscles produce heat, which must exit the body to prevent our core temperature from rising to dangerous levels. The body addresses this need by producing sweat, the evaporation of which cools the body. (Hard to believe, but during an hour of running you can lose more than two quarts of sweat!) This loss of fluid through perspiration impacts bodily functions and, if not replaced, can lead to dehydration. Symptoms of dehydration can include dizziness, nausea, cramping and chills.

So, you get the point...drink, drink, drink. Well, yes and no. The flip side of the coin is over-hydration, which can result in the dilution of electrolytes in the bloodstream. This is a serious condition that can severely impact the normal functioning of the brain, heart and muscle tissue. The symptoms, surprisingly, can mimic dehydration and, in extreme cases, can be fatal. Your best bet is to spread your drinking out during your long runs and your marathon and be sure to include electrolyte-replenishing beverages in addition to water. The International Marathon Medical Directors Association recommends drinking no more than 8 ounces of fluid every 20 minutes during a marathon. Dr. Liz Applegate, Nutrition Editor for Runner's World USA, adds that "If you're large or very muscular, or running in warm conditions, your fluid losses may be slightly greater." In general, women are smaller, less muscular and sweat less than their male counterparts.

A good rule of thumb is to monitor the color of your urine as well as the frequency. Frequent urination as well as pale-colored urine are good indications of adequate hydration.

During long walks or runs greater than 60 minutes or on the day of the marathon itself, a supply of carbohydrates is also important to maintain energy levels. If not addressed, you may find yourself feeling a bit sluggish. This is where sports drinks can edge out water, by replenishing those fuel-efficient carbs as well as electrolytes, which aid in fluid absorption and muscle function. (Energy bars or gel packs will also do the trick but be sure to drink water along with them to help keep you hydrated.) Dr. Liz Applegate, Ph.D., Director of Sports Nutrition at the University of California, Davis, recommends selecting a sports drink that contains around 50-80 calories per eight ounce serving. Any more and the concentration of carbohydrates may inhibit fluid absorption.

It is important to practice drinking both water and sports beverages during your training so that you learn what amounts and what types work best for you.

fueling on the run

Good nutrition and hydration begin long before race day. In fact, the months you spend training your lungs and legs to go the distance should also be spent educating yourself about and practicing these two important lifestyle habits. Proper nutrition and hydration throughout the course of training will

MEMORY JOGGER...
"During our first marathon, we felt compelled to stop at every water station (that makes 26, doesn't it?)... as well as every Porta-Potty (surprise!). Considering the temperature that day didn't rise above 40 degrees, we probably could have done with a lot less fluid intake. Hindsight!"

ensure that you bring the best you have to your long distance training sessions and to race day itself.

Consider your long run a "dry run with fluids," your dress rehearsal before opening night, your Braxton-Hicks contractions before true labor (that may be a poor analogy!) Distance runs afford us the opportunity to see what works best for us. Much of what our bodies require in the way of hydration and fuel depend on body mass, metabolic rate, the intensity of the workout, the amount we perspire, as well as outside factors such as temperature and humidity. You will quickly learn whether that cup of java before the run or those gummy bears at mile 18 were just the boost you needed or more than your stomach could handle. Practice, practice, practice...and keep notes on how you felt following those long sessions, the amount and kinds of fluids and carbs you consumed before and during the course of the run and the weather conditions as well.

The following are guidelines that will provide you with a general idea of what to drink and eat the night before and on the day of your long training sessions and marathon.

The night before. The tried and true pasta party on the eve of most marathons has proven itself to be most beneficial to endurance athletes. Hydrate well up until the time you go to bed and be careful not to overeat late that night as it may impact your sleep.

The morning of. Your body will utilize some of that food energy while you sleep, so be sure to eat a simple breakfast. Toast, cereal, a bagel and/or banana combined with 8-16 ounces of water or a sports drink two hours before the race should provide you with sufficient energy to rev those engines. Remember this is not the morning to include fats and proteins in your breakfast menu, as they will not digest easily and could cause some stomach discomfort. Some marathoners (that would include us) also swear by that pre-race cup of coffee, as long as you chase it with water. Finally, be sure to drink about 16 ounces of sports drink or water one hour before the race. Select a sports drink with less than 8 percent carbohydrate content for better absorption as well as less risk of stomach cramping.

During the race. The general rule of thumb here is to consume no more than eight ounces of fluid every 20 minutes. Be sure, if possible, to alternate your choice of beverages at fluid stations. We found that by alternating water, sports drink, and water combined with a gel pack provided us with ample carbs and fluids throughout the course of our run. Consuming sports drinks and other forms of carbs will reduce the stress on your body by fueling the muscles and maintaining energy levels.

Recovery. Carb-loading (can be a combination of food and drink) immediately following your long walks or runs and marathon is critical for recovery to replace the glycogen stores that have been lost. The first four hours post-run are especially important, but remember to spread out your carbs over those hours rather than consume a large amount all at once. Also include a little protein as well in those post-run meals to assist in muscle recovery, and be sure to continue to hydrate throughout the rest of the day.

These tips should provide you with the basic framework of hydration and carb-loading your body will need for those long workouts. Remember your goal is not only to cross that finish line, but to feel good doing it and to rebound quickly. After all, you want to look your best at your celebration party that night, right?!

weight loss

"Food is an important part of a balanced diet."

–Fran Lebowitz

While we hope that it is not at the top of your list of "Reasons Why I Chose to Do a Marathon," many of us that begin this journey do so with at least some thought given to losing a few pounds. Although running is an effective way to lose weight, do not expect it to happen overnight. During the first few weeks of training it can even be a bit unsettling as you notice the scales creeping up, not down. Keep in mind that your body is working hard to build muscle and that muscle tissue weighs more than fat.

Some key strategies to encourage those scales to reflect your hard work include running at least 25 miles per week (including at least two runs of 90 minutes duration), eating five to six small meals daily, running fartleks and drinking plenty of water.

For the average runner, logging 25-30 miles per week requires a daily intake of 2,500 calories. Trying to lose weight by eating less and running more is not the solution. The body's metabolism will slow down if inadequately fueled and you will be sabotaging your own weight loss efforts. Instead, along with those miles you log, keep an eye on what you are eating and when. Eat a well-balanced and varied diet and consume the majority of your calories in the first half of your day. Eat a bigger breakfast and lunch and a smaller dinner, and be sure to keep plenty of high-carbohydrate, low-fat foods around for sensible snacking.

Spice up your weekly training with fartleks (love that word!), a training technique used by endurance athletes which alternates intervals of high speed or intensity with intervals of lower speed. Try incorporating 30-second bursts of speed every seven minutes or so into a training run. Not only will fartlek training help to improve your speed and endurance, but it can also help you lose weight faster than running at a steady pace. Needless to say, drink lots of water. Not only will it fill you up, it offers a healthy no-calorie substitute for juices and sodas.

Our advice is moderation in everything. If you just happen to get a craving here and there…go ahead and indulge. "I eat chocolate every day," says Applegate. "Runners are allowed up to 200 calories of their favorite treat daily." So don't deny yourself that Hostess Twinkie. After all, you've earned it!

lacing it up

- Eat more complex carbohydrates (such as whole grains, fruits and vegetables) and less simple carbohydrates (sweets and candy). Carbohydrates should comprise 50 percent of your diet.
- Opt for mono-unsaturated fats, such as olive oil, over poly-unsaturated, saturated and trans fats. Fats should comprise 25-30 percent of your daily caloric intake.
- At least 20 percent of your total caloric intake should come from protein, such as lean meat, fish and soy products.

- Take a multivitamin daily.

- Hydrate throughout the day with at least 6-8 glasses of water.

- Practice fueling on the run with water, sports drinks, power gels and/or high carb snacks.

- Do not make weight loss your goal; now is not the time to cut calories. You will find that as you become more fit, your body shape will change.

---

in someone else's shoes...

Nutrition tips:

➤ *"Instead of Power Gels, I eat two Fig Newtons every five miles during a marathon. That gives me the energy I need."*

– Beth Eidemiller, age 51

➤ *"The week before a long run or the marathon itself, I make a pot of spaghetti on Monday and eat it for lunch throughout the week. Thursday I have a steak for dinner, and the night before the run I have pasta."*

– Natalie Mumford, age 29

➤ *"Don't ask me about food...I consider M&Ms a good breakfast!"*

– name withheld by individual's choice

---

one woman's story

When asked, most of us would rather not share some of the nicknames we earned in high school, but Paula Bruchhaus of Lake Charles, Louisiana, answers with candor. Stump. Standing five feet tall and wearing size 16 plus clothes, Paula waged a battle with her weight for over 35 years. Until January of 2002 at 4:35 a.m. to be exact. That's when she took action.

As a fourth grade teacher and mother of two young children, Paula's only free time was in the early morning. So when Gigi's, a local health club, opened its doors at 5 a.m., she was there. Her plan was simple. First learn how to turn on the treadmill. Then walk. After three weeks of these sunrise sessions, Paula was able to jog slowly for 30 minutes.

It may have been for the challenge or may simply have been for the tee shirt, but Paula entered and completed a 5K race. After scanning the crowd for someone more out-of-shape than herself and suppressing her fear of finishing last in front of the police escort, she tightened her laces and began. A myriad of races and a drawer full of tee shirts later, Paula realized her quest for fitness was not about what she had lost (70 pounds!) but what she had gained. Confidence.

Six months after her first foray onto the treadmill, she heard the word "triathlon" mentioned in the gym. Why not? As she stated herself, she could "swim across the pool as long as she had her big face-mask goggles" and she had "learned to ride a bike as a toddler."

Not only did Paula complete the mini-triathlon, but two months later she challenged her students to meet their Accelerated Reader class goal. The reward? She would enter the Gatorman Triathlon, an event including bike riding, swimming and a 4.5 mile run. The day they met their goal, this teacher lived up to her word. She filled out the registration form, signed her check and sent an eager pupil to the school mailbox. The morning of the event, seven expectant faces showed up to cheer their Mrs. Bruchhaus on.

On December 31, exactly one year after making the commitment to change her life, Paula stopped by to thank one of the fitness instructors at Gigi's. She couldn't verbalize her gratitude, but certainly her unadulterated tears spoke volumes.

Needless to say, Paula Bruchhaus learned the pay-off from taking risks. And more adventures lay ahead. In October of 2003 she down-loaded a training schedule from the internet and set her sights on a marathon. Only this time, she wasn't doing it for herself. Along with the little hands and super sized hearts of her fourth-graders, she ran to raise money for a sick baby in her community. And after countless 5 a.m. jogs, quite a few disappearing toenails, and a bet with one student's father for a class pizza party, she did it. Was there ever any doubt?

Those 26.2 miles showered Paula with a sense of accomplishment and a lesson that would last her a lifetime. She says it best in her own words, "Not too shabby for an old stump who feels like she's grown into a strong Live Oak tree."

over the coffee cup

Paula's first marathon: Houston Marathon

Age: 37

Time: 4:22

Q: What was the reaction of your friends and family when you decided to run a marathon?

A: Once my father stopped laughing (I was never athletic in high school), he became my biggest fan. He and all his friends at work tracked me (via the internet) during the race. He was very proud.

Q: Did you train alone or with a partner?

A: I trained alone with the companionship of my MP3 player. I love my music when I run.

Q: What one thing did you do right during your training?

A: I stayed true to my training schedule, and I had a reason to run—Baby Amber.

Q: What one thing did you do wrong?

A: I began the marathon at too fast a pace, zigzagging in and out of people. I stumbled and hurt my knee.

Q: Did you ever hit the wall?

A: At about mile 20 I felt I couldn't continue, so I reached into my pocket and pulled out a photo of the baby for whom we were raising money and a "strength angel" medal given to me by a friend. Seeing that baby with an I.V. and tubes connected all over her tiny body helped me to put things into perspective. My pain was temporary; hers was uncertain. I made it to the finish line, and I still carry that picture in my purse today.

Q: Do you have a million dollar trade secret?

A: Buy a poncho from the Dollar Store to wear in the beginning of the race; as you warm up, you can simply throw it away.

Postscript: *Paula's enthusiasm is contagious. Just ask the Prien Lake Elementary Running Club, which she created to encourage children to pursue fitness and exercise. More than 70 students meet weekly, keep running logs and earn prizes from community sponsors such as Wal-Mart. I guess you could say Mrs. Bruchhaus had a very cool idea and ran with it.*

Running Log

	Day 1	Day 2	Day 3	Day 4
Date				
Distance				
Time	Week	11		
Path/Notes				
Date				
Distance				
Time	Week	12		
Path/Notes				
Date				
Distance				
Time	Week	13		
Path/Notes				
Date				
Distance				
Time	Week	14		
Path/Notes				
Date				
Distance				
Time	Week	15		
Path/Notes				

Part 4

it's a girl thing

**"Obstacles are put in our way
to see if we really want something
or we just thought we did."**
-Anonymous

From Wendy's journal -

March 15, 2004

This past Saturday we ran 16 miles. Running distances naturally lends itself to much introspection, but in accomplishing a feat of this degree I had to rely upon mental strategies and consequently soul-search deeper than I ever anticipated.

There are so many broken people in this world. We all see them. Not just the homeless man rummaging through trash, but the church committee leader whose grown child broke her heart. She hides her sorrow behind crisp linen suits and manicured nails every Sunday. The factory worker who placed his own dreams on hold to better the future of his children. He knows his daughter's coat is frayed but hopes it doesn't matter in her eyes. People fighting mental illness. Men who don't feel respected and women who feel too old to be called beautiful anymore.

We probably all have a degree of brokenness in our own lives, present or past. But I have found that to dwell on it is a costly mistake. For every disappointment, there's a victory. For every tear, there's a smile. And during this last run, I visited a place where sweetness blanketed the ground and forgiveness floated in the air. I ran beside my father.

Daddy died nearly 10 years ago. He wasn't perfect. He was a broken man himself. But Saturday I realized that we are all composites of our experiences, good and bad. We are many things. And just as I will always be a child of alcoholism, I will also be a recipient of this man's humor that was so bizarre and so outrageous that it had to brand me with a signature of uniqueness. Daddy used to wear one red tennis shoe and one yellow one. When others commented that they "liked his shoes," he would routinely respond, "I have another pair just like them at home." It was this ridiculous sense of humor that perhaps sustained him through the horrors of the Battle of the Bulge in World War II. It was also this strange slapstick sarcasm that became my Crayolas in an otherwise black and white memory book. He was a character that could laugh at himself. He was a man of enormous strength. He was broken on the inside, but in his children's eyes, he could lift the world.

Saturday I envisioned him beside me. And I didn't feel like a victim; I felt like a victor. He always told his children that we could do anything we set our minds to. The moment I announced to my family that I was planning to run a marathon, it hurt when I received doubtful reactions. It hurt because I was conditioned to always getting a positive one. My Daddy would have been telling his friends that I already ran the race! His belief in his children was fantastic. There would have been no hesitation in his voice and no doubt in his mind. It was that man who ran with me Saturday. And I could feel the legacy he gave me. I could smell sweet potato pies; I could feel the shade of pecan trees; I could see magnolia trees graciously dropping their leaves. I could feel Virginia dirt between my bare toes in Daddy's garden right before sunset.

I know this is part of my heritage. Not only the unbreakable work ethic of a big, fat man with a host of broken dreams, but a father who hugged us in the only way he knew. With the smell of magnolias and autumn leaves burning and all the other gifts tendered by a tiny farm warmed by a southern sun and a belief that we could do anything we set our minds to.

chapter 9

attitude is everything:

facing your fears & overcoming obstacles

The boogey man, the dateless Saturday night, the "real world" facing you straight out of college, entertaining the boss, never finding Mr. Right…these are but a few of the fears we all encounter as we travel life's path. What we learn as we conquer each of these fears is that we cannot let these worries influence our decisions or determine our destinies. As Franklin D. Roosevelt so aptly stated, "We have nothing to fear but fear itself." (And perhaps the occasional blister!)

Many of you will find doubt creeping in while first entertaining the notion of completing a marathon. You will have reservations about your capabilities as an athlete, you may have concerns about budgeting the time for training, you may even have worries about the fundraising aspect of training with a charity. All of these should be given thoughtful consideration but never awarded "boogey man" status.

fears

Ability. "I'm not an athlete." We all have an inner athlete waiting to be unearthed…trust that you do too. Afraid you're too heavy, too old, too uncoordinated? Don't be! Just as women do, marathoners come in all shapes, sizes and fitness levels. Testimony to this is evident in each of our "One Woman's Story" sections. We trust that you'll find someone a little older, a little heavier, a little busier than you that has already faced that fear and moved beyond it. And if you don't, perhaps it's time you set the bar for others.

Time. "Where will I find the time?" Afraid that time will be an issue? We need to talk…all or most of us struggle to get done all that needs to be done in a day. The thought of squeezing in several hours each week for training may not seem plausible and, in fact, may seem a bit selfish. Let's rethink that perspective. Julie Isphording, former Olympic marathoner, equates the myriad of responsibilities that we all manage to a juggling act. She suggests "your responsibilities can be classified as either rubber balls (housework, volunteering, yardwork) or crystal balls (health, dreams, promises to oneself, family). If you drop the rubber balls there is no harm done. But the crystal balls need to be kept high in the air to keep them from shattering." View your running as a crystal ball, a precious gift to yourself of alone time that fulfills your need for relaxation while also providing innumerable health benefits. Granted, if you are a novice athlete, your first month of training may not seem to be a great form of relaxation! A long, soaking bath may seem the better answer! But we can assure you that as your running progresses, you will discover the healing powers of the sport, its meditative quality, its rejuvenating influence, its ability to cleanse the mind and body. You will discover a renewal of self that flows into all areas of your life. So let those rubber balls drop if you must but keep those crystal ones up high. Make that time. You owe it to yourself.

Fundraising. "I want to help, but…" For those of you who choose to train with a charity team, you may find yourself battling qualms about your ability to fundraise. We certainly did…but not for long. First of all, charities want you to succeed and most of them have built-in support programs to insure that you attain your monetary goals. Secondly, and even more important for you to know, is the amazing response you will undoubtedly receive from family, friends and coworkers. These worthwhile causes are typically incentive enough and, when coupled with your willingness to run 26.2 miles, they will be all you'll need to inspire generosity in the hearts of others.

Distance. "26.2 miles?" Pretty daunting, we know, especially on those first few runs when you can hardly make it to the end of the street without keeling over. Keep in mind, you're a work in progress. "You have to have dreams to make them come true," says Julie Isphording, "but dreams don't come true without a plan and a schedule." Looking ahead on your training calendar can be overwhelming, but trust that each week's regimen will prepare you for that weekend's long run as well as the next week's sessions. As you make your way through each week of the schedule (there's something so satisfying about crossing each day off with a highlighter!) you will begin to see that this process is taken one step, one day, one run at a time.

You may also develop a true obsession with distances and will undoubtedly find yourself checking your odometer each time you get into the car and doing the mental math. Let's see...one round trip to the mall plus a side trip to the park, over to the market in the neighboring town and back and that would be...what...just 16 miles...yikes! Yeah, we're all guilty. It seems, until we start training, we give more thought to the time it takes us to get somewhere than to the mileage. Trust us, you will become a bit of a fanatic, a virtual MapQuest of your community. No longer will it be 10 minutes to Loretta's house; it will be 1.2 miles!

All of this is your mind's way of comprehending the task ahead. Trust your training calendar and take one day at a time, one week at a time, one month at a time. Soon those 26.2 miles will begin to seem well with your reach.

obstacles

Track and field athletes are skilled at leaping hurdles as they circle the track, barely flinching if their toes clip and topple one of the wooden hurdles, their eyes focused on what lies ahead and not behind. You too will encounter these hurdles throughout the training, and you will learn to respect the challenge they present without letting them slow your course.

physical obstacles

For those of us that are fitness-challenged, let us dispel the myth that you will have the lion's share of physical obstacles. All of us have our own unique body composition and genetic makeup. We each will experience our own set of physical challenges. For some, the aerobic demands will be the greatest challenge, for others it will be muscular endurance. Age and body type certainly play a factor but not in one's ability to complete the marathon; rather in how the body and mind adapt during the course of training and the unique set of challenges they may have to overcome. For any athlete, the key is to listen to and respect what your body is trying to tell you. (You may have to tune out the whining, however!)

Injury. Stop, listen, learn. When, and there will undoubtedly be a when, you experience an unusual ache or pain, recognize it as your body's red flag. Too often these symptoms, if ignored, can result in more serious injury. Refer to our injury prevention chapter when you suspect a problem and, if necessary, contact a sports medicine specialist. We suggest the best antidote for minor injuries is to STOP and rest, something that is not always easy to do. Many novice runners fear that taking a reprieve from their training will get them off track and prevent them from meeting their goals. They continue to run through pain and then find themselves sidelined for even longer periods of time. The more quickly you LISTEN to and heed your body's warning signs, the more quickly you will find yourself back out there running.

LEARN from your injuries. Many early mishaps are the result of overtraining or the use of improper or old footwear. Follow the guidelines provided in your training calendar and resist the temptation to go farther or longer than recommended. Suitable, quality footwear will be your greatest guard against injury. Be sure to review the information on footwear in Chapter 6 before making that all important purchase.

in someone else's shoes...

Biggest obstacles faced during training:

➤ *"Time. With a part-time job and active teens, finding the time to do enough running was a challenge…especially when you're as slow as I am."*

– Cristine Fields, age 47

➤ *"I'm very social, so when we had long runs scheduled for Saturdays, I had to forego a couple of Friday afternoon Happy Hours and just keep Saturday as my night on the town."*

– Lauren Neufelder, age 28

➤ *"The biggest obstacle for me was the people around me. I had zero support. There wasn't even anybody saying that I couldn't do it, so I could use that as inspiration. No one had the least bit of interest! So I just kept it to myself. Eighteen weeks of training with only a book as coach and motivator. However, my friends and family did go to the race. They expected to see just a couple of people and a pavement chalk starting line. After parking two miles away and taking a taxi to the start, they wondered why the city was having a big festival downtown that early in the morning. Not once did they equate the "festival" with the race…until the end. By that time, they were really caught up in the excitement… "Are you going to run one next weekend?" they asked.*

– B.J. Rossback, age 36

Neglecting to stretch properly following a workout is also an invitation for injury. Consider the time you spend stretching as preventative maintenance. It's also a wonderful form of relaxation and your muscles will thank you for it.

Injuries can also be the result of poor form that a novice runner develops when first beginning to train. Most of us have a natural running style, one that feels comfortable and requires little thought. The biggest mistake would be to tinker too much with the natural rhythms of our bodies. On the other hand, if injuries continue to plague you, it might be a good idea to have a coach work with you to tweak your technique. Chapter 4 also offers basic tips on form that will prove helpful.

Cramps. Menstrual cramping (dysmenorrhea) can be an obstacle for female athletes, although many claim that walking or running actually helps to lessen their discomfort. The cramping we experience during the menstrual cycle is brought on by chemicals called prostaglandins, which cause the uterine muscle to contract. These contractions reduce the amount of oxygen in the uterus which can lead to cramping. Aerobic exercise may increase the body's supply of oxygen by improving blood flow and may also elevate levels of "feel good" hormones know as endorphins. If you still feel sidelined by cramps, consider taking pain medication such as ibuprofen, naproxen or acetaminophen to relieve the discomfort. Take a regular dose with food an hour before running and continue to use through the course of your cycle. Many women also find that cutting back on caffeine, sweets and salty food helps to diminish their menstrual discomfort.

Inclement weather. Over the course of a five month (or longer) training period, most of us will be exposed to a variety of weather conditions, some less than ideal. Look at those blustery, rainy, bone-chilling or humid days as a preparation for anything Mother Nature decides to dish out on the day you are scheduled to complete those 26.2 miles. Chances are it won't be a day blessed with idyllic weather conditions. Your many training sessions, however, should acquaint you with the challenges as well as the pleasures of the many variations in wind, precipitation, temperature and humidity and will provide invaluable experience in coping with those challenges. If conditions are hazardous (icy sidewalks, subzero temperatures), consider moving indoors to a track or treadmill, but don't avoid the outdoors unless absolutely necessary. There are important lessons to be learned from braving those elements, not the least of which is layering. You will quickly learn the wisdom in layering and discover the beauty of neckwarmers, headbands, gloves and hats.

Nonetheless, even the best prepared of us can be fooled by Mother Nature. Amazingly, in all of the months of training for our first marathon, we never ran in the rain. As Murphy's Law would have it, we awoke to torrential rains and a temperature of 40 degrees on race day morning. A close friend provided us with plastic ponchos, which were helpful in keeping the rain off of our upper body but proved cumbersome and awkward in which to run. Without any head cover, the icy rain quickly transformed us into drowned rats (what were we thinking blow drying and styling our hair that morning?) Our shoes soaked up twice their weight in water and our drenched clothing became a breeding ground for blisters. Having never encountered these conditions during training, we were woefully unprepared and suffered the dismal consequences. The moral: expect the best, but prepare for the worst. Hopefully your marathon day will be more temperate than ours!

Nature calls. Okay, this may not be up there in your top list of obstacles, but, not surprisingly, it is a concern for most women. Your long walks or runs will provide you with invaluable experience for marathon day. First, be sure to allow yourself sufficient time beforehand to "take care of business." Allow time for that cup of coffee and energy bar to move through your system before you leave for your training sessions and empty your bladder just before heading out the door. Rest assured, there will be porta-potties along your marathon course, but you may not be so fortunate on your practice runs. Know in advance what facilities will be at your disposal along the route. Despite these precautions, you will probably encounter a time or two when you just can't wait another minute. Ladies, that's when you may just have to take it to the woods. Marathoning is not a sport of vanity and, in a pinch, you sometimes do what ya gotta do. Trust us, you won't be the first!

We must also mention a final reminder when packing for race day—Kleenex (can serve double duty). Although porta-potties line most marathon courses, they may not always be adequately furnished with all the necessities. Be prepared.

mental obstacles: "I think I can...I think I can..."

That Little Engine that Could sure set a wonderful example for all of us growing up, and what about that little old ant that thought he could move that rubber tree plant? Everyone knows an ant can't...well, you get the picture. Chapter 9 will provide you with some of the more tried and true cerebral exercises that athletes use to will their bodies to new limits. These tricks and tips will be ineffectual on marathon day, however, unless practiced routinely throughout the course of your training. Start experimenting early to find those that work best for you.

Same old, same old. Although the entire process of training for a marathon will provide you with new challenges on a daily basis, you still need to safeguard against boredom. That ho-hum mentality can best be addressed by changing your routines on a regular basis. Map out and explore new routes, run with a new friend or group, even try training at a different time of the day. After weeks of early morning runs where you and the moon seem to have the world to yourself, it's incredible how stimulating it can be to run as people are returning home from work. (Good visibility has its benefits; you'll be rewarded with a symphony of horns and encouraging waves from friends who spot you along the way!) If you haven't tried it before, try training with music; if you have, then change the selections. Vary your turf and move to the soft soil of a dirt trail or even take it inside to a treadmill or indoor track on occasion. Like any great relationship, you can't let your training get stale…mix things up and you'll keep it alive.

The nay-sayers. In the early stages of training many of you may get reactions from friends, family and coworkers that are less than supportive. Julie Isphording, accomplished runner and Health Reporter for WVXU in Cincinnati, refers to these people as "energy vampires" that will "suck you dry." They will tell you all of the reasons tackling a marathon is a pipe dream, they will question your motives, your sanity and your ability. Your response should be a simple "just watch me" accompanied by a confident smile. Save the "I told you so" for after you cross the finish line! Support may heighten as your significant others watch you continue to train and develop as an athlete. Yet you may always find that your own enthusiasm far exceeds that of those on the sidelines. Remember, the goal you have set for yourself is an enviable one. It is a lifetime achievement that many would never dream of attempting, and they may harbor some jealous sentiment. The key here is to adopt the "when, not if" attitude that kept us moving towards that finish line. (WHEN I complete the marathon, not IF I complete it!) That show of confidence should be enough to keep the doubting Thomases at bay. Surround yourself with positive and supportive friends and training partners and keep in mind the following wisdom shared by Mark Twain: "Keep away from people who try to belittle your ambition. Small people always do that but the really great make you feel that you, too, can become great."

hitting the wall

Bonking, or hitting the wall, frightening words that can strike fear into the hearts of even the most fearless, are terms you will undoubtedly hear many times during the course of your training. In a nutshell, they refer to that dreaded (but certainly not inevitable) state of energy depletion that can stop a runner in her tracks. It is a virtual roadblock of the mind, the body or both, and it is brought on by a depletion of bodily reserves of glycogen. It typically occurs around mile 20, the point at which most runners have drained their carbohydrate fuel tank. As evidenced by a quick glance at your training calendar, the closest run you will encounter prior to the full marathon distance of 26.2 miles will be your 20 miler.

Subsequently, you will probably not be pushed to the point of bonking during the course of training. That's a good thing…we suppose. On the other hand, fear of the unknown can be paralyzing and can set you up for unnecessary anxiety come race day. "Forewarned is forearmed," they say, so let's dissect this angst-inflicting state of being.

First, let's define bonking a little more clearly. Carbohydrates provide the energy we need to fuel not only our muscles, but our brains as well. As they enter the body, carbohydrates are converted into a usable form known as glucose, which travels throughout the body via the bloodstream. The liver removes the glucose it needs to fuel the brain and the remainder is absorbed by the muscles. Both the liver and the muscles have a maximum storage capacity, however, so any residual glucose is stored as fat. (Although fat does serve as a reserve source of energy, it is not as efficient in its delivery.) As we run, our muscles and brains begin draining these energy stores. If not continually replenished, the body begins to shut down. Research has shown that it is most likely the brain that signals "empty" even before we have truly depleted our muscle glycogen stores. Mind over matter…not always in our favor.

So how do we best equip ourselves to avoid crashing into that proverbial "wall"? Preparation is key. Your long walks or runs will be a great source of training in more ways than one. They will teach the body to gradually use fats, that back-up source of energy we mentioned earlier, to extend the duration of your limited carbohydrate stores. Practice makes perfect in all aspects of marathoning.

Additionally, you can increase your odds of breaking through that wall by pacing yourself from the beginning of the race. Too often, we tend to "go out fast," energized by the enthusiasm of the cheering crowds and the subsequent adrenaline rush that often accompanies that exhilaration. Just as our automobiles run more fuel-efficiently when we keep our odometer at a steady speed, our bodies run most efficiently when we maintain a steady pace throughout the marathon. Of course, expect to slow down a bit on particularly hilly parts of the course. Don't push to maintain the same pace that you would run on flat stretches or you could also speed up the depletion of your energy stores.

Finally, and perhaps most importantly, feed your brain throughout your walk or run. Supplement those body stores with carbohydrate-rich sports drinks or gels and water and you will most likely scale that wall instead of crashing into it. More recent research has also shown that proteins consumed during the course of the race may help to increase the absorption of blood glucose by the muscles, thereby enhancing the energy efficiency of carbohydrates and ultimately conserving muscle glycogen and improving endurance. You might want to experiment with some of these carbohydrate-protein drinks (Accelerade,

Endurox R4) on your long runs. If they have a significant impact on your energy, they may be just the answer for you. So if you want to keep those legs moving and that brain from talking you out of finishing a race you are more than prepared to complete: don't skip out on those long walks or runs, maintain a steady pace and be sure to refuel throughout the walk or run.

lacing it up

- Don't second guess your ability to complete the marathon.
- Prioritize the time needed for training.
- Rest assured that your fundraising will be easier than you imagine.
- Trust the training schedule to prepare you adequately to complete all 26.2 miles.
- Heed the messages of your body; don't ignore aches and pains, but rest and seek treatment if necessary. Also remember to stretch.
- Be prepared for unpredictable weather conditions.
- Be prepared when "nature calls."
- Vary your training regimen enough to prevent boredom.
- Surround yourself with positive people, not nay-sayers.
- Know that "hitting the wall" is not inevitable. Learn to practice proper pacing and fueling on your long distance jaunts.

one woman's story

She didn't like what she saw—that person in the mirror, that young woman staring distantly back at her with a resigned downward turn to her smile. It was a youthful face that struggled to mask the emptiness she felt inside. It could have been easy to miss, but on closer look, she saw it… just a snatch, just a glimpse, but she clearly saw it in those eyes. A glimmer of hope, a pleading almost that reached out and spoke with such clarity: "Don't give up on me." She couldn't ignore it. She had spent a lifetime listening to others, why not to this voice.

Bettie Coen had grown up in a home that did little foster her dreams…no encouragement, no expectations, no promise of a better future. She married young, divorced young and found herself alone with two small sons to raise. Financial hardship found her entangled in an abusive relationship, dependent on a man who chiseled away at the little self-esteem she still clung to. And yet she stayed, reconciled to the life that seemed her destiny. Until the day that quiet voice whispered back to her in the mirror…the same day that she realized she was too young to grow old.

Bettie laced up a pair of sneakers, headed outdoors and began to run. She ran to recapture the youth that her body had lost, she ran to escape the destruction of her relationship and she ran in search of a better tomorrow—for herself and for her sons. It was a gradual process for Bettie. She slowly shed the pounds, she eventually ran three miles without stopping, and little by little, she began to take control of her life.

In running, she uncovered a self she'd never known before. She also discovered a group of people unlike any she had met before. People who were kind and good and encouraging, people in charge of their lives, people she wanted to be more like. It was while watching the runners at the Denver Marathon one cool fall morning that she saw something familiar in the eyes of her new friends as they willed their bodies towards the finish line—that same recognizable whisper of determination that she had heard so many months before. The next day and for many days ahead, Bettie found herself on a greater quest than she had ever dreamed possible. She began to train for a marathon.

Just 10 weeks later, she crossed her own finish line and she never looked back. One month later she packed up her things, strapped her sons into their car seats and left behind the abusive relationship. With a renewed confidence and perspective on life, she found herself writing to the president of Bonne Bell, applying for a job with a company for which she had little background experience but whose philosophy she embraced: beauty comes from within. She shared with him her story and belief that her experience as a competitive runner offered a great foundation for a position on his sales force. A runner himself, Mr.

Bell understood the discipline, the self-motivation and the steely determination that governs marathon athletes. He gave her the job. She created her future.

Bettie likes what she sees in the mirror these days—that twinkle in her eyes no longer just a whisper. She knows that her reflection is exactly that…a reflection, of the beauty, the confidence and spirit that lies within.

Postscript: Bettie went on to build a successful career for herself and a bright future for her two sons. Her marathon, a defining moment in her life, was the first step along a path that has been marked with many more accomplishments. Following her sons' graduation from college, she went back to school to complete her degree and graduated Summa Cum Laude from the University of New Mexico in May of 2004, nearly 25 years after her first marathon. She continues to run five to seven miles daily and has competed in several triathlons. With a Bachelor's degree in Spanish and her love of that culture, she has also discovered a passion for flamenco…keep dancing, Bettie!

over the coffee cup

Bettie's first marathon: Denver Marathon

Age: 34

Time: 3:45

Q: What was the reaction of your friends and family when you decided to run a marathon?

A: My sister was so supportive, and all of my friends were tirelessly supportive—my phone rang and rang the night before as friends called to wish me well.

Q: What were your biggest obstacles you encountered during the course of your training?

A: Scheduling the long runs. My boyfriend resented the activity (I never wanted to be with a jock) and later accused me of having an affair. You betcha—I was falling in love with long-distance running!

Q: What was the one thing you did right during training?

A: I followed a sensible training plan, and I ran three 20 milers before the race, then tapered.

Q: What was the one thing you did wrong?

A: Not starting my running career many years earlier!

Q: Did you ever hit the wall during the race?

A: Not in my first marathon. I learned about that in my second one while pushing myself to test my capabilities. I ran it in 3:08 and it hurt like crazy!

Q: What is your advice for first-time marathoners?

A: Just do it! Establish a good running base (usually a minimum of one year of consistent weekly mileage). Then follow a prescribed training program. Run the first marathon for fun. Just finishing is a realistic goal. Enjoy, enjoy, enjoy.

Q: Do you have a million dollar trade secret?

A: It's all in the preparation. Do the training and then run your plan. A balanced diet and rest are also important.

Q: What life lessons did that first marathon give you?

A: That anything is possible and it is never too late to make your dreams come true. The marathon taught me that I could take charge of my life, that I could be the mistress of my destiny. The lessons I learned have made it possible for me to do and accomplish things I would have never dreamed possible before running 26.2 miles.

chapter 10

left, right or scatterbrained? mental tricks

Nobel prize winner Roger Sperry initiated the study of the relationship between the brain's right and left sides. Physicists have discovered parallels between the human brain and Einstein's quantum universe. Complex tests have been devised to determine the relative dominance of the two hemispheres of an individual's cerebral cortex. We, on the other hand, simply suggest that walking to your bathroom and examining your tube of toothpaste is the best litmus test of all in determining if you are right-brained or left-brained. And if you can't even find the toothpaste, it is evident that you fall into the third category, the one with which we are most familiar, scatterbrained.

Back to the toothpaste. It has been said that if the tube is ever-so-neatly rolled up from the bottom, you are more than likely left-brain dominant, keeping company with mathematicians, analysts and neuroscientists. If the tube looks squeezed at random, perhaps by someone's toes even, then you are right-brain dominant, joining the ranks of poets, artists and eastern yogis. Why is this important to a marathoner-in-training? Because as distances increase, you will need many mental tools at your disposal to fight the roadblocks of boredom, pessimism and discomfort. Understanding how you think and learning tricks to improve your cognitive frame of mind and thus your performance will reap benefits you cannot imagine. Can you complete those 26.2 miles without reading this chapter? Probably. Will you be less likely to succumb to unexpected obstacles along the way if you heed our suggestions? Definitely.

It is often said that a marathon is actually two races; the first 20 miles are run with your feet, the last 6.2 with your mind. We believe the entire distance calls upon the strength and willfulness of the mind, especially those steps from the safety net of your home to the trepidation of the starting line. Given two marathon hopefuls of similar training background—one strong of body, the other of mind—we would place our money on the latter.

tricks of the trade

To begin with, the common assumption that we are either right-brained or left-brained is false. We each have a whole brain (whether utilized fully or not) and can effectively train both hemispheres to perform certain skills more efficiently. The idea is to practice some cognitive exercises that will help keep you focused and also some that will keep you distracted during those long runs.

Analyze the course before running or walking it. If you are an analytical person who solves problems through the use of data and logical reasoning, this trick may work for you. Alyce, a logical thinker, insisted we drive the marathon route before race day. She made mental notes regarding hills, memorized landmarks at each five mile increment and familiarized herself with the landscape. (Admittedly, we also hunted for a safe spot to leave a cosmetics bag for touch-ups, but we never followed through.) She assigned family members and friends to specific mile-markers where she believed she would need extra motivation. She even drew a map of the course, charting elevation statistics. It gave her comfort to strategize and develop a game plan for race day, although she knew to expect the unexpected.

Concentrate on form. As fatigue creeps into your longer runs, your concentration and focus can weaken. Once of the first things to suffer is form. You begin to shuffle instead of run; your shoulders and arms become tense. Your breathing may even become irregular. When you notice these signs, make a conscious effort to regroup. Mentally divide your body into four quadrants. Start with the head, shoulders and arms. Be sure that your head is looking forward, eyes focused on the street/sidewalk in front of you. Relax your shoulders. Arms should be bent at a 90 degree angle at the elbow. Hands should be gently cupped and not clenched.

Now, mentally work your way down to your torso. Concentrate on breathing in a rhythmic pattern. Two breaths in and two breaths out is a comfortable rhythm for most runners. Pull your abdominal muscles inward.

The third quadrant includes your trunk and legs. Be sure that your hips are facing forward and your legs are relaxed and lifting those feet off of the ground.

Finally, be aware of how your feet are striking the ground. The pattern should be heel down first, roll forward through the arch and push off with your toes. Think light, not heavy. You will find that proper form helps you to exert less effort and makes it easier to finish your training session.

Disengage. Some athletes find it helpful to remove themselves mentally from the workout, and there are numerous ways of doing this. For example, problem solve. Distract yourself from the monotony by attacking mathematical problems. In order to finish the marathon in six hours, my pace needs to be how many minutes per mile? In order to feed 14 dinner guests, I need to make how many batches of chicken parmesan? And how many of us have done this mental tabulation? In order to shed 15 pounds by Joan's party, I need to lose how many pounds per week?

Make lists. Silently scribble down grocery items or pending errands. Jot down a honey-do list for the upcoming week. Make a wish list for plastic surgery procedures if you're truly desperate for a diversion! You can also perform this exercise with a group. A fellow runner shared that he poses challenges to his running buddies such as recalling as many songs as they can that mention the word "run."

in someone else's shoes...

Favorite mental tricks:

➤ *"I consider 13.1 miles the finish of the race. Then I just think I need to make my way back home. It is a lot easier than to think of it as half done."*

– Sandy Gitmed, age 66

➤ *"Talk about EVERYTHING!"*

– Sarah Drewes, age 22

➤ *"I dedicate each mile to someone important to me."*

– Tania Carter-Day, age 37

Plan your child's birthday party. Organize your thoughts for tomorrow's business lunch. Design a page in your scrapbook. Wendy documented her marathon journey in a scrapbook and received her best inspiration during long runs.

Visualize. If you consider yourself creative or intuitive, you write songs while driving in your car and your best poems are scribbled on grocery receipts, then you fall into the category of right-brain thinkers. You may find visualization especially effective. If training with a charity, visualize the person for whom you are running coaxing you to keep going. Visualize yourself crossing that finish line, the crowds cheering.

Use imagery to disconnect yourself from the thought of 10 more miles to go. Many athletes say that envisioning their legs as part of a well-oiled machine helps them drift into a trance-like state. Our friend Sara coached us up and down many hills by encouraging us to imagine our legs as wheels. "Let them roll, just relax and let them roll!" Of course, at the time, they felt like Flintstone boulders on Fred's car, but nonetheless the trick helped.

Converse. The art of conversation is magical. Play mobile armchair psychiatrist and analyze and resolve your companions' social dilemnas. Ask your training buddies' opinions on your romantic travails, work-related issues, politics, even make-up tips. After 25 weeks of training, you may just have all of the world's problems solved. Just beware of the gal who talks too much. If you train with a group, you'll no doubt encounter a Chatty Kathy, and that incessant banter becomes tiresome. (That's when you fake an ankle sprain and insist that she continue on without you.) An ideal partner is someone who gracefully balances the need for interaction with the need for quiet. A secret of all marathoners is that nothing is more cathartic than a little solitude. You will come to treasure those peaceful interludes when mixed with adequate doses of social interaction.

Self talk. This exercise is helpful for both right and left-brain thinkers. When the going gets tough, talk yourself through it. Just as we respond to comments others say about us, we react to messages we tell ourselves. If you constantly remark to others that you are slow, you will begin to believe that about yourself. Why not fuel your mind with positive statements? "I am disciplined. I am sticking to my schedule. I am not afraid of hills. I am getting stronger every day. I am doing something I never dreamed I could."

Many athletes have a favorite mantra that carries them up steep hills or through trying moments, such as "drop the shoulders…relax…breathe" or "I will not walk this hill…I will not walk this hill." As silly as it may sound, pack a few positive mantras into you repertoire of mental tricks to call upon during particularly challenging moments. When the time comes for that extra push, pull one from your hat and don't be afraid to chant it aloud. Your positive exclamation may be just what the girl behind you needs to hear as well.

Another soothing practice of many long distance athletes is prayer. A long run or walk on a brisk day has a way of cleansing your mind. Use the quiet of such times as a spiritual retreat from busy schedules. Pray or meditate. Alyce found that praying the Rosary was a soothing escape during high mileage jaunts. When faced with a difficult climb up a foreboding hill in a race, Wendy often resorted to singing her children's Bible songs. Not on tune, however, but with heart, soul and sweat of course.

Be creative. We were fortunate to train on Saturdays with a group of girls in their twenties. They not only made us feel young, but they were quite imaginative. They suggested we each scribble several thought provoking or fun questions on strips of paper to keep in our pockets. At boring intervals during long runs, we would take turns posing them to one another. What television character are you most like and why? What is a nostalgic smell from your childhood? If on Survivor, who in our group would be voted off first? (Is your mind already wandering?)

practice, practice, and then practice

As with any skill, executing these mental tasks takes practice. By the time your distance training reaches beyond seven or eight miles, you should consciously rehearse these mental tips and tricks. You will soon discover which ones work best for you and those you'll want to use on race day.

Finally, we encourage all of you, no matter which side of the brain dictates your thinking, to daydream about race day. Imagine the finish line, the crowds, the noise. Imagine the tears, the pride, that medal around your neck. Imagine the arms of someone you love and a victory no one can take away from you...ever.

lacing it up

Practice using mental tricks during long distance training sessions. Determine which ones work best for you.

- Analyze the course before race day.
- Improve your concentration skills; focus on form.
- Practice disengagement with problem solving, list making and day dreaming.
- Practice visualization; use imagery to keep you going.
- Enjoy good conversation.
- Practice positive self talk.
- Be creative with games to play along the route.

one woman's story

How appropriate that an accomplished runner began her quest to complete a marathon in each of our 50 states in beautiful Hawaii, the fiftieth state to join the union. How remarkable, too, that 26 years after completing that memorable first, this 61-year-old woman is still running marathons. And how ironic that it all began one spring day in 1979 as Franceska Drozdz was enjoying a cigarette on her front lawn and just happened to look up in time to spot a small group of people running by in their "underwear…"

Ten years earlier, 24-year-old Fran bid a tearful farewell to her husband of just 11 months. A pilot, he was headed to South Vietnam on a tour of duty with the U.S. Air Force. It was not the honeymoon she had imagined and yet she knew what she had signed up for when she married this handsome, young pilot. She knew that settling down was not in the cards for the wife of a military man. But she vowed, as she watched his plane taxi down the runway, that it would be the last time she would be left behind.

Upon his homecoming one year later, the youthful couple departed together for a four year assignment in England. A year after their return home, they welcomed a baby girl into their lives and with little Amy still in diapers, Uncle Sam called once again. The young family packed up and headed off, stroller in tow, to yet another island, this time in the Pacific—Okinawa, Japan.

Five years and far more than five pounds heavier, Fran and her family island-hopped once again, this time returning to their beloved homeland. Although not a part of the continental United States, they were thrilled to be stationed in Hawaii and to feel the comfort of American soil beneath their feet. What a place to begin their welcome home party—on this beautiful tropical paradise. It was an easy place to grow complacent, to grow lazy in the warmth of its sunshine, to spend languid afternoons outrunning waves with their daughter on the crystalline Aloha beaches.

...As she stamped out the embers of her cigarette into the lush grass beneath her feet, Fran struggled to contain the grin evoked by the passing of those scantily-clad runners. She laughed aloud when she heard that they were part of an annual "Fun Run"—an oxymoron if she'd ever heard one. An amusing sight, yes, but also strangely enticing. Despite their comical attire, it was evident from the smiles on their faces, this group of people were indeed having fun on their run.

Not one to let a good time pass her by, Fran laced up an old pair of sneakers and joined a running group that trained at the nearby University of Hawaii. Undaunted by the fact that her only prior running experience was chasing after a bus, Fran threw away her cigarettes and threw herself into her training, which she admits she confined to the darkness of the night or the pre-dawn hours of the morning. Not only was it unfashionable to sweat at that time, she admits her greatest fear was subjecting her neighbors to the sight of an overweight woman jogging past them in her undergarments! As part of her training regime, Fran joined a weight loss group and three months later and several pounds lighter, she completed the prestigious Honolulu Marathon.

Little did she know that that milestone was just the beginning. The beginning of a new life for herself and of a life devoted to inspiring others to modify their behavior, to lose weight and to wake up with a purpose. Not only has Fran kept off those extra pounds, she's also kept running. After spending a good portion of their life outside of the United States, she and her husband of 37 years are today traversing their own country as Franceska adds one more notch to her marathon belt with each state they visit. They are finally shaking hands with their homeland, getting to see the America they so dearly love and bringing a smile to the faces of those people standing on their lawns watching a 61 year-old woman run by in her "underwear."

What a wonderful life, what a splendid honeymoon.

Postscript: *Francescka completed her fortieth marathon (the Yakima River Canyon Marathon in the state of Washington) in April 2005. She is a member of the "50 States Marathon Club" and the "50 States and D.C. Marathon Club," two prestigious organizations whose members include runners who have completed marathons in at least 10 different states. For years she has also traveled across the country as a motivational speaker and has helped to organize groups to participate in the well-known Race for the Cure to fight breast cancer. Two highlights of her life include her selection to carry the Olympic Flame for the 1984 Los Angeles Olympic Games as well as the 2002 Salt Lake City Games. What a wonderful and proud example of the great American spirit!*

over the coffee cup

Q: What advice would you offer more mature women who are considering running for the first time in their lives?

A: I've encountered many women my age that have run marathons, and I attribute it to surrounding ourselves with high energy people instead of those who would discourage us.

Q: Does your husband share your passion for running?

A: My husband is my greatest supporter; I couldn't do it without his encouragement. He walked his first half-marathon in Des Moines last September (2004) and is going to walk the Fargo half-marathon next month (2005).

Q: Can you offer one bit of advice for someone running her first marathon?

A: Stay away from nay-sayers and surround yourself with like-minded people.

Q: As a motivational speaker, is there one quote or adage you live your life by that you could share with our readers?

A: I get great strength from the quote from Hebrews, "Let us run with endurance the race that is set before us."

Q: How long did it take you to complete your first marathon and what has been your overall best time?

A: I ran my first one in over five hours. I didn't know what I was doing and stood in long long lines to go to the bathroom, etc. I t wasn't until I ran 20 marathons that I finally GOT IT! My best time was 4:00:18. It killed me to watch the clock turn from 3:59:59 to 4:00!

Running Log

	Day 1	Day 2	Day 3	Day 4
Date				
Distance				
Time		Week	16	
Path/Notes				
Date				
Distance				
Time		Week	17	
Path/Notes				
Date				
Distance				
Time		Week	18	
Path/Notes				
Date				
Distance				
Time		Week	19	
Path/Notes				
Date				
Distance				
Time		Week	20	
Path/Notes				

Part 5

girlfriends in their glory
"Life isn't a matter of milestones but of moments."

-Rose Fitzgerald Kennedy

From Wendy's journal -

March 17, 2004

Countless books I have read on marathons all repeat the same message: "No one who has run a marathon is ever the same person… your life can change in a single step…you discover new strength and you learn to trust it…"

I have been pondering this for months, wondering when that magical moment will arrive, when all that I have invested in this project will culminate…when I will finally learn that bit of truth that will change my life…

I think I have the answer. The magic is not wrapped in a single moment. The learning has been gradual. The lessons will not be presented to me like a long awaited diploma. They have been unfolding for the past six months. And the "truth" referred to in so many books is really just a chance to see ourselves as we truly are. Our strengths and our weaknesses. And this takes courage.

Training for this marathon has forced me to see myself realistically, not ideally. As a middle-aged woman, brave enough to test the limits of her physical and mental strength, and wise enough to know that there are demons to fight along the way. The messiness of life…the surrendering of youth, compromised dreams, a reflection in the mirror we're surprised to see that is ours.

Throughout my training, I have been forced to face this woman in the mirror. I have learned to appreciate her weaknesses, because they allow her to grow. And I have learned to recognize her strengths, because they help define her.

Mostly, on this journey of self-discovery, I have been taught that life is too short to fill our days with people who are not on our "mentor committees." I choose, instead, to surround myself with friends who are inspirational human beings. My teammates have shown me this. Friends who make us want to do better, to be better.

I guess that's what I've learned. So if some magic pops up the moment I cross that finish line, it will merely be icing on the cake.

chapter 11

decompression: the importance of tapering

What words can better instill fear in the hearts of women than "only 21 shopping days left until Christmas!" As intended, they invoke frenzy among even the most laid-back of our gender, hurtling us out the door and into a whirlwind of others similarly driven to complete a seemingly endless list of shopping. No different, we suppose, than that three week deadline the boss has given you to come up with a deal-making advertising campaign for your largest client! How about the last month of your pregnancy when you suddenly realize everything that still needs to be done before that precious bundle of joy arrives, the invitation that arrives in your mailbox three weeks before your twentieth class reunion, that last minute announcement that the in-laws will be arriving to pay you a visit…is your heart racing yet?

It's true, most of us have understandable issues with those final weeks leading up to a big event. We tend to kick into overdrive, muscling every ounce of energy we have in store to "get things in order" before the big day. Well, toss those worries aside, girls. You are getting ready to enter the 21 most satisfying, gratifying and energizing "leading-up-to-the-big-event" days of your life! It's TAPER TIME!!

Time to chill, lay back, enjoy the fruits of your labor. Believe it or not, that may be easier said than done. As mentioned above, we are conditioned to dig down and bring all we have to the plate when we're approaching a much anticipated event, especially one in which we have invested so much of ourselves. How do we put the brakes on when we've been driving at full throttle for so long? The better question might be—how can we not?

why taper

We have called upon our bodies to go the extra mile (literally and figuratively) for several months, and these last 21 days are all about payback. Our bodies have not only earned a break, they need one in order to meet the physical and mental demands of marathon day. Taper time allows your muscles to replenish carbohydrate stores, repair tissue damage and to reduce fatigue so that your body is well rested and strong on race day.

when to taper

Most experts, including Karen Cosgrove, Cincinnati-based coach for the marathon training program Team in Training, recommend that the tapering period begin as soon as you've finished your last long distance training session. In our program, this is the 20 mile run, scheduled three weeks prior to marathon day.

countdown: week 1

Training. Your training calendar will map out for you the specifics of this first week of tapering in terms of mileage, weights, cross training and hill training. Note that your mid-week session is reduced by 15 minutes and your long session this weekend is less than half of what it was the previous week. The rest of your schedule remains much the same.

Mind. As your body adjusts to less rigorous demands, your mind will gladly pick up the slack. This is a fun week as you begin mapping out strategies for race day.

- Make or confirm travel arrangements. Even if your marathon is a local one, consider staying in a hotel close to the starting line. You will avoid traffic jams, street closings and parking issues. You'll also enjoy the luxury of some peace and quiet the night before that can be difficult (if not impossible) to get at home.

- Make plans to attend the pre-race pasta party and expo held the night before most marathons. These events are fun and give you the opportunity to meet other athletes, check out the latest running equipment and stock up on a host of freebies!

- Study the course map on the race website and familiarize yourself with the starting line, the halfway point and the finish line. Look for landmarks, fluid stations and, more importantly, Porta Potty locations! If you are fortunate enough to live close by, take the time to drive it. This familiarity with the course will help you next week as you practice some visualization techniques.

- Make a mental list of problems that have arisen before, particularly on your long runs or walks (i.e. blisters, IT band discomfort, shoes laces coming untied, sweat in your eyes, runny nose, etc.) Decide now how you will prepare for and tackle those problems—bandaids or creams (BodyGlide works wonders), lightweight braces, double knotting those shoelaces, sweatbands, tissues. Add those just-in-case items to your packing list. (Amy Bruno, a marathoner from Minnesota, wipes away sweat with a baby wash cloth she always tucks into her shorts pocket.)

- Set realistic time goals for marathon day. You should have some idea of your race pace following your 18 and 20 mile runs or walks. (Note: our only goal for our first marathon was to maintain or surpass a 15 minute mile pace, because race coordinators warned that the streets would be reopened to traffic beyond that pace. We couldn't bear the humiliation of being demoted to the sidewalks!)

Body. This is still an active week by anyone's standards. The tapering period is a slow and gradual transition so that you maintain your muscular and cardiovascular endurance while allowing the body to begin critical repair work.

- Shoe shopping. (We knew you'd love this one!) Unless you've recently purchased a new pair of running shoes, this is the ideal time to do just that. If you have not experienced any problems with your current pair, then play it safe and purchase a second pair of the same brand. If aches or injuries need to be addressed, seek the guidance of a professional at a specialty walking/running store. Begin wearing your new shoes this week, beginning with short distance runs, and they should be comfortably broken in by marathon day.

- Nutritionally, this week, it is especially important to include a lot of protein in your diet to aid in the repair of the muscle tissue that has been damaged during the last several weeks of training. Continue to eat wisely and keep your diet well-balanced. This is not the time to be cutting calories despite the decrease in your weekly mileage.

- Take stock of those feet that will be carrying you the distance in just a few weeks. Trim your toenails and attend to any blisters that have crept up in recent weeks. Unless troublesome, leave those hard-earned calluses alone until after the marathon; the pedicure should come later!

- Continue to stretch those muscles. Stretching will help lessen your risk of injury during training prior to the big day. Tip: while lying down in bed, legs slightly elevated, practice using your feet to air-trace the alphabet. This helps to stretch and strengthen your ankles.

- Go ahead. Get your hair done. You've got finish line photographers awaiting your arrival!

countdown: week 2

Training. You will notice a marked decrease in total mileage this week. Two weekly sessions are reduced by 15 minutes each and your weekend long run is only six miles. (Do you remember the day you thought six miles was a long run?) You will also notice this week that you will no longer be doing any weights or cross training; use those days to rest instead. Don't be tempted to cheat. Your rest is critical and gives you more of an edge than any extra miles or lifting would impart now.

Mind. You may find yourself getting a bit restless this week with the significant reduction in training. Keep yourself occupied with some of the following:

- Continue to practice the mental tips and tricks that have worked for you in the past so that they are second nature by the day of the marathon.

- Continue to check the race website for any updates or additional information that may prove helpful on race day.

- Practice visualization. Lie down, put on that headset and, as you enjoy your favorite background music, picture yourself at the starting line. Practice relaxed breathing as you envision yourself taking off at a controlled pace. Imagine yourself hitting your stride and gliding past the crowds, favorite landmarks, beautiful scenery. If you have already walked or run part of the course, focus on those stretches that were challenging and use this time to think about how strong you will feel after you have completed those segments. If you are unfamiliar with the route, use your course map, website photos, written descriptions and your imagination to guide you through this mental process. Continue this relaxation technique throughout the next two weeks.

Body. Well into this second week of tapering, the body is still hard at work repairing muscle tissue that was damaged during the high-mileage phase of your training. Therefore, it is crucial to keep eating as though you are still in those intense last weeks. This is not the time to cut calories. Keep eating a balanced diet with the recommended ratio of carbohydrates, fats and proteins. Each of these nutritional components serves a unique purpose during this time of rest and recovery. Not only will good dietary practices help hasten repair but they will also work towards building necessary reserves of energy for your big day.

countdown: week 3

Training. Hard to believe, but your combined miles this final week of tapering will be less than half of what your long session was just two short weeks ago! Cross training is curtailed, weights are wiped out and hills are history. Your body should be starting to appreciate this rest phase, and you should feel refreshed and ready for the big day ahead this weekend. Ready to kick up those heels?

Mind. Remember those butterflies in your tummy the week before school started or the flip-flops your stomach turned waiting for your first date to arrive? You might find yourself feeling like that young, fidgety school girl again this week. Anticipation can be a conflicting emotion. One moment you are overcome with feelings of giddiness, the next you are struggling with pangs of anxiety. Take comfort in knowing that these are predictable and desirable emotions. Your giddiness will gift you with understandable enthusiasm (look what you have already accomplished and what you are getting ready to achieve!) Your anxiety will reward you with that adrenaline rush many athletes credit for giving them a competitive edge. If you find yourself feeling especially anxious, stop and remember that the last 24 weeks have more than prepared you for this big day… be confident in your training.

- Rent some motivational/inspirational movies – *Cool Running, Rocky, Flash Dance, Rudy*. Kick back and let those video heroes pump you up. (Then remind yourself that you're the real thing.)

- Continue with your visualization practice and keep it positive. Picture yourself crossing that finish line, arms held high, your friends and family cheering you on. (Can you feel those goose bumps yet?)

- Make a list and start packing that suitcase or overnight bag. Now is the time to set aside your race day clothing, bib and timing chip (these are included in your race packet you will probably pick up at the expo), shoes, socks and whatever else you plan to carry with you on the race. Consider a shirt or shorts with small pockets that will allow you to tote lightweight necessities such as bandaids, tissues, gel packs, etc.

- Prioritize yourself. Save the vacuuming, partying and traveling (other than to your race destination) for another week. This is the week to catch up on your sleep, sneak in a long soaking bath, listen to soothing music and delve into a good book. Pamper yourself. (Note: sex can be a great form of relaxation therapy this week, but conserve your energy the night before the race!)

Body. Those nutritional balance scales should tip in the direction of carbohydrates this week, bumping up to about 70 percent of your total caloric intake during the three to four days prior to the race. Hydration is equally important. Keep water and sports drinks readily available and drink until your urine is clear. Don't overdo it though. Excessive hydration can result in "water intoxication" or hyponatremia, a rare but hazardous condition that occurs when blood sodium drops to dangerous levels. Sodium is essential for maintaining water balance in the body as well as aiding in the normal functioning of organs and muscles. A handful of salty pretzels here and there and making sure to balance your water intake with sports drinks (which supply necessary electrolytes) will help to offset this risk.

Hope you enjoy your tapering! You have earned it. You are a machine! Physically and psychologically you have willed your body to exceed personal limits each successive day, week and month for the last 22 weeks. You have probably never felt as confident, fit or accomplished as you do right now. Be proud of yourself. We certainly are!

lacing it up

- During the first week of tapering, confirm travel arrangements, familiarize yourself with the course and prepare for anticipated race day problems (blisters, etc.).
- During the second week of tapering, continue to employ mental tricks during training and practice visualization.
- During the final week of tapering, find avenues for relaxation and reflection, continue to practice visualization and pack your overnight bag.
- Be sure to eat a well-balanced diet; now is not the time to cut calories.

one woman's story

She sees it every day in the eyes of her patients, a will to live and a fight to make it through one more day. As a busy oncologist and hospice medical director, Gerry Ann Houston spends her days doing battle alongside her patients, delivering not only the medical expertise that her long years of schooling have provided, but imparting as well her philosophy that we can do anything we set our minds to do. She knows more than most how to make each day count. It is exactly that appreciation and zest for life that first brought this accomplished woman to the starting line of a marathon.

Raised on a dairy farm, Gerry Ann grew up watching her father rise before the sun to milk his 100 cows and then return to the fields after breakfast to prepare, plant or harvest his land. It was only after a second round of milking that he would at last head home to enjoy an early supper with his growing family. Despite the demands of farm life, he refused help from his children during the school year, insisting their time was better spent on their studies and the leisure he believed belonged to the young. There were no days off for her dad, no family vacations either—cows didn't go on vacation, after all. Yet it was an idyllic youth. Summer mornings were spent cleaning the milking parlor alongside dad, but lazy afternoons meant riding horses or catching a wagon ride down to the creek, where she and her younger brother and sister would cool their toes and busy themselves with the imaginings of a child. The acres of farmland and woods provided them an ample playground to run and play, to while away their days and to dream wistfully of their futures.

Those lazy days of her childhood melted away as Gerry Ann worked towards her dream of becoming a doctor. Three years of undergraduate school, followed by four years of medical school, three years of residency and two years of a fellowship left little time for anything but studies. Gerry Ann later joined a busy oncology practice in Jackson, Mississippi, and she and her husband, a radiologist, enjoyed any free time they had with their young daughter. It was in preparation for a much-needed skiing vacation that Gerry Ann took up jogging in her early thirties. She enlisted a good friend and neighbor to join her three mornings a week before work and came to appreciate the quiet camaraderie they shared before the rest of the world opened their eyes. Years later, at the gentle urging of another close friend, Gerry Ann reached for yet another goal, one that seemed lofty to even this accomplished woman…running a marathon.

It was during her months of training that Gerry Ann saw clearly the metaphoric link between her running and the long roads her patients travel during their battles with cancer. The aches and pains, the grueling uphill battles, the uncertainty of what lies ahead, the blessed comfort of a friend by your side. Every one of her patients run their own marathons, along seemingly endless stretches of road, willing themselves to go the distance and making every step, every day count. Gerry Ann understands. She learned, at a young age, the precious gift that life is and how quickly it can be snatched away…she was only 16 when her father passed away. Gerry Ann still goes back to visit that farm of her youth, hiking the woods and dipping her toes in the creek. She often finds herself in quiet conversations with her dad, thanking him for all that he taught her…to rise early, to work hard and to never give up. But his response is always the same…life is short, make time for yourself and time for your family. No, cows don't take vacations and neither do patients. But Gerry Ann has learned to. She has also discovered the priceless gift of an early morning run when one can witness the birth of yet another precious day.

Postscript: *Dr. Gerry Ann Houston completed her first Boston Marathon at age 46, the same age of her father when he died. She has completed a total of five marathons and was honored in 2003 to ride the final 40 miles with Lance Armstrong in the Tour Of Hope in Washington, D.C. She continues to run and has also taken up biking, frequently doing century rides. She plans to climb the Grand Tetons for her next adventure.*

over the coffee cup

Gerry Ann's first marathon: Marine Corps Marathon, Washington, D.C.

Age: 44

Time: 4:14

Q: What was the reaction of your friends and family when you decided to run a marathon?

A: Everyone wanted to know why I would even want to do something like that. But knowing me, they knew I would be able to do it.

Q: What obstacles did you encounter during the course of your training?

A: Finding time to train while working full time as a medical oncologist and being a wife and mother of a teenager.

Q: What was the greatest inspiration to you during this time?

A: As I did this as part of Leukemia/Lymphoma's Team in Training, I ran in honor of a very brave lady suffering from leukemia. Her battle was a much tougher fight than my training.

Q: What was the one thing you did right during your training?

A: I ran with a friend for the long runs. Having support from a training partner and keeping on schedule were essential.

Q: What was the one thing you did wrong?

A: I can't think of anything I did wrong. The weather could have been better, as it was cold and rainy the entire 26.2 miles.

Q: Did you ever hit the wall?

A: No. I paced myself and took in hydration and nutrition at the appropriate stops.

Q: What advice can you share with the first-time marathoner?

A: Develop a training program and stick to it. Train with a friend who runs at your same pace. Make finishing your goal, not a certain time. And most importantly, HAVE FUN.

Q: Do you have a million dollar trade secret?

A: No, I wish I did!

chapter 12

it's my party: race day & afterwards

Douglas Wakiihuri once told journalists, "Even if I explain [the truth about the marathon] to you, you'll never understand it, you're outside of it." Jack Lovelock philosophized, "Big occasions and races which have been eagerly anticipated almost to the point of dread, are where great deeds can be accomplished." And Jerome Drayton said that to describe a marathon "to someone who's never run it is like trying to explain color to someone who was born blind." What do these individuals have in common? They are all Olympians. How can their experiences possibly parallel the endeavor you're about to complete? After all, their finish line performances seemed flawlessly choreographed to camera flashes and cheering crowds. In the words of Julie Isphording, who broke ground as the first female member of the U.S. Olympic marathon team, "Why don't you believe that you're a champion too? The crowds are bigger [at the Olympics] but the crowds in your mind can be outrageously wonderful." These Olympians' treks across the finish line may have attracted greater fanfare than yours or mine, but the miles they ran still numbered 26.2. And as Julie adds, "Don't stop at outrageously wonderful." You are about to accomplish an incredible goal, and only you will be able to savor its true value, its gift and its indescribable color.

marathon eve

Evenings before special events in our lives are predictably exciting but can also be filled with anxiety. Keep yourself busy with the race day preparations listed below and you will do much to diminish those pre-race jitters. There is a calming effect to having everything in order and ready to go, so don't wait until the last minute.

- Marathon expo. Don't miss out on the fun. You will enjoy browsing through all of the exhibits and viewing the myriad of runners' gadgets and gizmos, filling your bag with free samples and just mingling with fellow athletes. (Tip: don't be tempted to try new items you pick up on race day; put them aside for future runs.)

- Race Packet Pick-up. Most often, you will pick up your race packet at the expo. Check with the online race website for details. Your packet will contain a variety of items, but most importantly your bib number, specific race day information and a timing chip.

- Pasta party. Traditionally, marathon events sponsor pasta parties on the evening before the race. Take advantage of this fun event—another wonderful opportunity to meet fellow participants who will share in your excitement. (Tip: some events may require reservations; plan ahead.)

- Plan your outfit. Take time to lay out your race day outfit on your bed along with all necessary supplies. If your bib number has a tear-off strip to record emergency contact information, be sure to fill it out prior to pinning it to the front of your shirt. Use the list below as a checklist of items you will want to consider taking with you tomorrow:
  - Shirt (with racing number attached)
  - Shorts
  - Gummy bears
  - Sunglasses
  - Bandaids
  - Kleenex
  - Runner's watch

- o   Headband, hair items

- o   Water bottle, plastic

- o   Skin lubricant

- o   Sweatpants, t-shirt (discardable)

- o   Running shoes

- o   Socks

- o   Ibuprofen

- o   Disposable camera

- o   Cash

- o   Car key (lace through shoelaces)

Note: Consider dropping your room key off at the hotel front desk when you leave for the race. The night before, arrange for a wake-up call and ask if late check-out is available.

- **Mapping it out.** Verify directions to the starting line, make arrangements to get there (friend, shuttle, walk), confirm meeting times and places with partners and read through the information in your race packet. And don't forget to hydrate, especially after the pasta dinner. We would also remind you to get a good night's sleep, but that is usually impossible the eve before such a momentous event. Don't worry; you've got the rest of your life to catch up on sleep!

marathon day

- **Wake-up.** Set your alarm clock at least two hours before the start to give yourself plenty of time to eat, hydrate and stretch. As mentioned in Chapter 7, keep breakfast simple, such as a bagel, banana and water. A cup or two of Gatorade or similar drink is a good idea as well. If you are used to a particular item, such as a cereal bar or oatmeal, bring it with you to the hotel.

- **Lotion-up.** Sounds silly, but you'll thank us later. Apply a skin lubricant, such as Bodyglide, to all places susceptible to chafing—feet, thighs, under arms. And if the weather forecast is sunny, don't forget the sunscreen.

- **Dress-up.** Steal one last glance at the weather station and dress appropriately for predicted temperatures. Will you need that rain poncho? A top layer of old sweats that can be easily discarded? And don't forget your race chip!

- **Warm-up.** A brisk walk from the hotel or parking lot to the starting line is a convenient way to warm up those muscles. Plan to arrive 30-45 minutes prior to the starting time to allow for last minute bathroom breaks.

- **Fuel-up.** You may want to carry a water bottle with you the first few miles of the race to avoid the crowds at the fluid stops. Remember to keep a controlled, steady pace in the beginning. (A useful trick is to dissect the race into three segments; think about your pace the first 10 miles, your form the next 10, and pull those mental tricks from your hat for the final 6.2!) Also, don't forget to hydrate and fuel properly throughout, alternating sports drink, water, and gel with water. Don't eat or drink anything on the course that you haven't tried in training.

- **Wise-up.** Remember race day etiquette. With all the hubbub and excitement, it is easy to forget the rules of the road. Keep these following tips in mind for a safer and more enjoyable experience for everyone.

  1) Start smart. Line up according to your race pace. Unless your pace is record-breaking, this will mean the middle or back of the pack. Keep in mind, your chip time will not begin until your feet cross the official starting line.

  2) Don't stop, drop and roll. Do not stop in the middle of the road, especially in those beginning few moments of the race. If you drop something, let it go and keep moving! That first half mile can often resemble the infamous Running of the Bulls. A sudden stop and you are apt to be trampled or cause someone else to take a tumble. If you need to stop to walk, drink, fuel, lace your shoes or (heaven forbid!) spit, move to the side of the road to avoid a collision or pile-up.

  3) Two-By-Two. When running with a group, do not run more than two abreast. A Red Rover-like line can be frustrating to others wanting to pass.

4) Coming Through. A simple "excuse me" or "coming through" is a common courtesy to extend when you are the runner wanting to pass. This heads-up to your fellow runner will be much appreciated and may just spare you an elbow in the stomach.

5) Smile Every Mile. Offer fellow runners some words of encouragement along the way and promise yourself to share at least one smile every mile. Bet you'll get more than twenty-six in return!

MEMORY JOGGER..."After hearing numerous tales of emotional encounters along the race course with other participants, running angels who will you to go those last few miles and breathe inspiration into your every step, I tried enthusiastically to strike up conversation with passing runners. I longed to make just such a life-long connection with someone partaking in this same sentimental journey...but to no avail. After a few minutes of meaningless chit-chat, they'd leave me behind with a perfunctory 'Have a good one!' Disheartened, it dawned on me: at mile 10, drenched with rain and numb from the cold, I accepted a coat from a generous onlooker...a size XXL onlooker who stood at least six feet tall (I'm a size six petite). Wearing this ankle-length yellow parka, I realized that apparently no fellow marathoners wanted their finish line photos with Sponge Bob!"

in someone else's shoes...

Race day tips:

➤ *"If you want people to cheer for you, write your name somewhere on your clothing or body. At warmer marathons, if I'm running in a sports bra and no shirt, I'll write my name on my stomach. Having 50,000 cheerleaders at Boston was awesome!"*

– Jennifer Quarles, age 33

➤ *"During the race I play a little game. I select a person in front of me and I make it my goal to pass him. Then I pick out someone new."*

– Beth Eidemiller, age 51

➤ *"I carry Ibuprofen in a tiny plastic bag I found in the pharmacy (Ezy Dose® pill pouch). It keeps them dry and is much lighter than a pill case."*

– June Williams, age 49

➤ *"What did I do with my medal? Of course I wore it to bed the first night...doesn't everyone?"*

– Nancy Shura-Dervin, age 54

6) Finish Forward. When you cross that glorious finish line, remember to keep moving forward through the chute and stay in the order in which you crossed the finish line.

it's your party

The race is over, but your work is not. Remember to utilize the following tips in order to speed your recovery.

- Hydrate right away. You need to replenish the fluids that you have lost.
- Start refueling immediately. Eat whatever carbohydrates are available to raise your lowered blood sugar levels. Also consume protein, as it aids in tissue repair.
- Stretch.
- Wear that medal proudly.
- When you arrive home, opt for a lukewarm or cold bath over a hot one.
- Wear that medal proudly.

(Did we say that already?)

what next?

Not quite the same as post-partum blues, but the post-marathon experience nonetheless begets its own share of nostalgic ambivalence. One friend confided in us that a few weeks after her marathon debut, she frequently found herself sentimentally rummaging through her drawer full of running clothes. Eventually the singlets and racing shorts won out, as she felt herself summoned back to the sidewalks to train for her second race.

But don't think this marathon fever will only take you across more finish lines; it can take you to entirely new horizons. Some running enthusiasts accept the challenge of completing marathons in all 50 states, such as the members of the *50 States & D.C. Marathon Group*. They definitely put a new spin on distance running. And if this isn't adventuresome enough, you can always follow Joe Hale's lead. This Cincinnati executive who was born to a mother immobilized by polio set his goal for 7 in 7 on 7. Seven marathons, that is, in seven months on seven continents. And while dashing around the world, he surpassed his goal of raising $100,000 for the March of Dimes.

Finally, if your quest for thrills is still not satisfied, you can always sign up for an ultra-marathon. That's right, a race that's *longer* than a marathon. We would give you more information on this sport, but the mere idea of running a

30, 40 or even 50 mile race stops us dead in our tracks. You're on your own for this one, girlfriend!

Not everyone will feel a calling back to the marathon circuit, and this is permissible. You've done it already! The unfathomable. And once a marathoner, always a marathoner. You may even decide to channel your energy into a different direction. Now that you've been inducted into the world of running, you might find yourself becoming more competitive. Shorter races, such as a 5 or 10K, are excellent opportunities to work on increasing your pace. If you enjoy distance training, you may find the thought of a half-marathon enticing but another full one too arduous. That's fine, too. The important thing, however, is to periodically sign up for races of some sort if you plan to continue your walking or running regimen. Having these short term goals will help keep you disciplined.

Now that you've unearthed your inner athlete, are you ready to tackle a different challenge? Add some diversity to your athletic portfolio? You may fall prey to the lure of the popular triathlon. Since its Olympic debut in the Sydney 2000 summer games, triathlons have grown in popularity and in number across the United States and the world. The triathlon seems to be a common progression for many marathoners. One appeal of this sport is the wide range of types. A triathlon is an endurance race composed of three different sports, usually swimming, cycling and running. Some more innovative ones may include canoeing or even snow shoeing! There are mini-triathlons, sprint triathlons, the half Ironman and the ultimate challenge—the full Ironman, which consists of a 2.4 mile swim, 112 mile bike ride and (believe it or not) a 26.2 mile run. Consider joining the growing number of triathletes in the U.S., as it is an excellent tool for embracing new sports. You may compete in only one triathlon, but in doing so, discover that swimming is your new passion.

Whether your marathon experience leads to new athletic endeavors or keeps you close within its ranks of loyal runners dotting the sidewalks in the early morning, our hope is that it will open up other areas of exploration for you…of all types—athletic, academic, social and spiritual.

More than likely, you will discover the relationship you developed with your neighborhood running trails is one too precious to give up completely. Shift gears and focus on speed if you want to take your running to the next level. If not, slow down and earmark your jogging for pleasure only. Just make sure you don't "outrun your joy of running," as Julie Isphording advises. Remember, no one sets the rules but you. You listened to your heart once and traveled down a truly exciting path. *Keep* listening, and who knows where the road might lead.

parting words from wendy

Unless you've skipped multiple chapters, by now you've probably become somewhat acquainted with me through my journal excerpts and scattered essays. Hence, you've probably also drawn the accurate conclusion that I am a foolishly sentimental woman who undoubtedly cries while watching Disney movies. But surprisingly, my parting words of wisdom to you have nothing to do with tears. Rather, the words I want you to carry on these last 26.2 miles of your journey have everything to do with laughter—have fun.

The day before my first marathon was hectic, not at all the calm and pensive one for which I had hoped. It was also a memory that will color my youngest son's childhood for many years to come. I spent the day cutting, stitching and assembling a hot pink pig costume for him to wear on race day. And the next morning while I was trying to achieve one of the most intimidating goals of my life, Eric was enjoying celebrity status on the sidelines of Cincinnati's sixth annual Flying Pig Marathon as the funniest, most original and certainly most loyal little pig I had ever seen. Marathoners stopped in their tracks when they spotted him and pleaded for photos; I couldn't wait until I reached mile 17 to see my offspring in action; and he ended the day by darting onto the race course and running the final yards across the finish line beside me. And to think, I had never thought a pig could make me cry.

Recently I traveled to Virginia Beach to accompany my sister in her first marathon. I promised I would walk beside her the whole way, as she celebrated her fiftieth birthday by undertaking such a formidable quest. Because the majority of our four siblings, six nieces, four nephews, seven great nieces and nephews, a cluster of in-laws, and a slew of cousins, aunts and uncles too numerous to count reside in that area, we hoped for at least a small following of supporters to surprise us on race day. No such luck. Easter egg hunts and a Sears white sale won out. There we were. Two middle-aged women amid a gathering of elite athletes in an ocean side hotel, wondering what the heck we were doing…so we made a sign. "OUR LAZY-A** FAMILIES DID NOT COME. WILL YOU CHEER FOR US?" Okay, I assume full responsibility for this lapse in propriety, but such tackiness paid off. We held our sign high when passing pockets of bystanders, and we were applauded by everyone. Onlookers, officials and even other race participants called out our names (plastered across the front of our shirts, of course) and cheered us on. Old women, skate-boarding teens and camera-laden tourists all related to our primitive message. A bit of laughter proved priceless for everyone.

I am fond of a piece of advice offered by Mae West. "Between two evils, I always pick the one I never tried before." Don't take yourself so seriously, girlfriend. Enjoy life. And above all else, have fun.

– Wendy

parting words from alyce

> **"When I stand before God at the end of my life,**
> **I would hope that I would not have**
> **a single bit of talent left and could say**
> **'I used everything you gave me.'"**
> **– Erma Bombeck**

Inspiration, that wellspring of hope that provides us with clarity and vision and often guides us from darkness into light. It can come in the beautiful simplicity of the first crocus to show itself in springtime, in a simple quote taped to an office bulletin board, in the softness of a watercolor's pastels. It can be found in a simple melody, in a breathtaking mountaintop view or in the tranquil rhythm of waves crashing into the shore. But I have learned the greatest source of inspiration is most often found in the lives of those around us and in the moments that surround us.

I have found it in the gutsy determination of a woman who struggled to win her battle with cancer and in the victorious smile of a young boy who did, in the grace and dignity of a family who have weathered unimaginable pain and in the tireless devotion of a mother to her special needs child. I have seen it in the sacrifices of families who have suffered through financial hardship, in the eloquence of a child's prayer and in the strength of a young widow raising her children alone. I have felt it in the tranquility of a long morning run with a best friend and in the simple pleasure of an evening spent with treasured friends. I have seen it in the beauty of a daughter's eyes, in the wisdom of a mother's words and in the patience of a husband whose wife is writing her first book.

These are the people and the moments that inspire me. They are the people that choose, by how they live and how they handle what comes their way, to embrace life and to live it to its fullest. They are the moments that encapsulate the richness of life's simple pleasures. They are my inspiration, the moments and the people in my life, all within arm's length.

I hope that you, too, will find inspiration within the pages of this book and in the stories of the remarkable women included therein. They are women, just like you, who have chosen to redefine their lives and have used the gifts they have been given to do just that. More importantly, I hope that this book will open your eyes to the world of inspiration that lies just beyond your front door.

- Alyce

one woman's story

The perfect gift—that elusive acquisition that often leads us on an exhaustive and, at times, disheartening search of the shelves and racks that line our favorite stores. The ideal purchase that, in its perfection, will convey to the recipient his or her significance in your life.

It was in anticipation of her mother's upcoming birthday that Wendy Whipple found herself in search of just such a gift. Somehow, the cashmere sweater, the best-selling novel, the silver bracelet of years past were not the gifts she sought this year. Perhaps it was that, as a young adult, Wendy could clearly appreciate the beauty of the gifts that her mother had given her—the devotion, the encouragement, the belief that her dreams could come true. Perfect gifts. The realization that the best gifts often come without a price tag and always come from the heart was the inspiration behind the small package she placed in her mother's hands that year…

Karen Whipple describes her life as blessed, married for 40 years to a wonderful man whose career in the Air Force took them and their three children on an exciting journey across the United States and around the world. With each move Karen encouraged the children to get involved and she watched with delight as they explored and flourished in each of their new homes. She watched with pride as, over the years, they grew into involved and independent young adults. And she watched, with just a twinge of sadness, as the very wings she had given them also gave them flight, away from home, eager to map out their own futures and discover their own worlds.

... Karen smiled as she looked down upon the small package her daughter had placed in her hands. It was a simple package, holding no hint of what lay beneath the layers of brown paper and ribbon. Inside was a small slip of paper, a handmade calendar and a promise. The slip of paper – a prepaid registration form; the calendar – a marathon training calendar; and the promise – a pledge from Wendy to train by her side. At 54, Karen knew that the most priceless gift she unwrapped that day was in knowing that her daughter believed she could do it.

Over the next several months, mother and daughter embarked on a journey that held unspeakable treasures. Their training offered miles and hours of time together, to talk, to laugh and to share. Five months later, the family packed up once again and headed to Orlando for the Disney Marathon—a race selection Karen found poignantly appropriate. It was the place that inspired a great man to declare, "If you can dream it, you can do it." Walt Disney embraced that belief. Karen and Wendy ran with it.

The photos with Mickey and Minnie, the music and fireworks, the medals awaiting them as they crossed that finish line together cast a spell on that day that Karen will never forget. Those were among the most memorable gifts they took home. But it was the magic in knowing that their journey together as a family was just beginning and in her daughter's unwavering belief that she too could fly, on the very wings she had given her children, that was the best gift of all. It was, indeed, the perfect gift.

Postscript: Karen and Wendy have kept the magic alive by completing four more marathons together. Karen's husband and youngest daughter, Kerry, were inspired to complete a half marathon at Disney the following year. The year after that, son Chris joined Karen and Wendy to run the Chicago Marathon. Now that's a family with wings!

over the coffee cup

Karen and Wendy's first marathon: Disney Marathon, Orlando, FL

Time: 5:51

Q: What was the reaction of your friends and family when you decided to run a marathon?

A: (Wendy) Our family was excited to be a part of it—they were going to come watch. Mom became an inspiration to others without even knowing it.

Q: What were your biggest obstacles you encountered during the course of your training?

A: When we started training, it was July and very hot in Memphis. After those summer months, we were able to go longer without much trouble. We also made sure our routes went past public restrooms.

Q: Who was the greatest inspiration to you during training?

A: Each other. We were in this together!

Q: What was the one thing you did right during training or the race?

A: We took walk breaks every 15 minutes. It helped on our recovery the next day.

Q: What was the one thing you did wrong?

A: We drank too much water the day before. We were going from porta john to porta john the first half of the race.

Q: Did you ever hit the wall?

A: Not really. We were tired and sore, ready for it to be over, but not ready to give up just yet.

Q: What advice can you share for the first-time marathoner?

A: Take it one step at a time. If you just keep putting a foot forward, you'll make it eventually. Time means nothing compared to the accomplishment.

Q: Do you have a million dollar trade secret?

A: Run with someone you love! They may dislike you for a few miles, but they will always love you! (Wendy shared a cute marathon day story about her typically sunny-dispositioned mom: "…as we were running, I found myself shouting hello or something upbeat to people that passed us or those we passed. Around mile 18, I called out hello to someone and my mom muttered, 'Would you just shut up? No one wants to hear you anymore!'" We feel your pain, Karen.)

Q: What life lessons did that first marathon give you?

A: Set a goal, work hard and you can achieve it. The next few marathons won't be as hard!

Q: Do you have a race day tip to share?

A: Always carry a disposable camera with you on race day to capture those special moments.

Running Log

	Day 1	Day 2	Day 3	Day 4
Date				
Distance				
Time		Week	21	
Path/Notes				
Date				
Distance				
Time		Week	22	
Path/Notes				
Date				
Distance				
Time		Week	23	
Path/Notes				
Date				
Distance				
Time		Week	24	
Path/Notes				
Date				
Distance				
Time		Week	25	
Path/Notes				

training calendar

training calendar

	S	M	T	W	Th	F	S
week 1	weights/x-train	30 min. easy	weights/x-train	30 min. hills	30 min. easy	rest	40 min. long
week 2	weights/x-train	30 min. easy	weights/x-train	40 min. hills	30 min. easy	rest	4 miles long
week 3	weights/x-train	30 min. easy	weights/x-train	40 min. hills	30 min. easy	rest	4 miles long
week 4	weights/x-train	30 min. easy	weights/x-train	40 min. hills	30 min. easy	rest	5 miles long
week 5	weights/x-train	30 min. easy	weights/x-train	40 min. hills	30 min. easy	rest	5 miles long

It takes 30 days for a habit to form. Be consistent with your training.

Your cross training sessions should last 15-30 minutes.

You're strengthening bones & muscles now; cardio will come later.

"The miracle isn't that I finished. The miracle is that I had the courage to start." © John Bingham

	S	M	T	W	Th	F	S
week 6	weights/x-train	30 min. easy	weights/x-train	40 min. hills	30 min. easy	rest	6 miles long
week 7	weights/x-train	30 min. easy	weights/x-train	40 min. hills	30 min. easy	rest	6 miles long
week 8	weights/x-train	30 min. easy	weights/x-train	40 min. hills	30 min. easy	rest	7 miles long
week 9	weights/x-train	30 min. easy	weights/x-train	40 min. hills	30 min. easy	rest	8 miles long
week 10	weights/x-train	30 min. easy	weights/x-train	45 min. hills	30 min. easy	rest	9 miles long

When training in the dark, wear reflective attire.

Your cross training sessions should last 30-45 minutes.

Be sure to stretch after every training session.

"There are clubs you can't belong to, neighborhoods you can't live in, schools you can't get into, but the roads are always open." –Nike

training calendar

	S	M	T	W	Th	F	S
week 11	weights/ x–train	30 min. easy	weights/ x–train	45 min. hills	30 min. easy	rest	10 miles long
			Are you hydrating enough? Drink one cup of sports drink before each long session.				
week 12	weights/ x–train	30 min. easy	weights/ x–train	45 min. hills	30 min. easy	rest	12 miles long
week 13	weights/ x–train	30 min. easy	weights/ x–train	45 min. hills	30 min. easy	rest	12 miles long
			Your cross training sessions should last 45-60 minutes.				
week 14	weights/ x–train	30 min. easy	weights/ x–train	45 min. hills	40 min. easy	rest	6 miles long
week 15	weights/ x–train	40 min. easy	weights/ x–train	45 min. hills	40 min. easy	rest	14 miles long

Now is the time to figure out which items are best for you to use during the event. Are you familiar with Power Gel or Gu?

"Life itself is the proper binge." –Julia Child

training calendar

	S	M	T	W	Th	F	S
week 16	weights/ x–train	45 min. easy	weights/ x–train	45 min. hills	45 min. easy	rest	7 miles long

Practice mental tricks, such as visualization, on your long runs this month.

week 17	weights/ x–train	45 min. easy	weights/ x–train	45 min. hills	45 min. easy	rest	16 miles long
week 18	weights/ x–train	45 min. easy	weights/ x–train	50 min. hills	45 min. easy	rest	8 miles long

How are your shoes doing? Do you need a new pair? The best way to tell is to try on one new shoe and one old one. If the new one offers noticeably more support, it is time.

week 19	weights/ x–train	45 min. easy	weights/ x–train	50 min. hills	45 min. easy	rest	18 miles long
week 20	weights/ x–train	45 min. easy	weights/ x–train	60 min. hills	45 min. easy	rest	10 miles long

Your cross training sessions should last 60 minutes.

"Challenges are gifts that force us to search for a new center of gravity. Don't fight them. Just find a different way to stand." –Oprah Winfrey

training calendar

	S	M	T	W	Th	F	S
week 21	weights/ x-train	45 min. easy	weights/ x-train	60 min. hills	45 min. easy	rest	20 miles long
				Your cross training sessions should last 60 minutes.			
week 22	weights/ x-train	45 min. easy	weights/ x-train	60 min. hills	45 min. easy	rest	10 miles long
week 23	weights/ x-train	45 min. easy	weights/ x-train	45 min. hills	45 min. easy	rest	8 miles long
				Are you taking it easy during your tapering phase? Don't try to make up missed sessions.			
week 24	x-train/30 min. no weights	easy	x-train/ no weights	40 min. hills	30 min. easy	rest	6 miles long
week 25	rest	4 miles easy	3 miles easy	rest	2 miles easy	rest	26.2 miles
				Start loading up with nutrition and water. Carry a water bottle with you while traveling.			

"My grandmother started walking five miles a day when she was sixty. She's ninety-seven now, and we don't know where the hell she is." –Ellen DeGeneres

resource guide

apparel

One More Mile www.onemoremile.net : This is a great source for trendy running gear at reasonable prices.

Target retail stores: If your budget is limited, Target carries a nifty line of sportswear for women at affordable prices. We find the Prospirit™ line holds up well.

Road Runner Sports (www.roadrunnersports.com): This company's claim of being the largest online store for running gear just may be true, as you can even find microfiber underwear here! You can also shop for apparel by brand names.

Soark (www.soark.com): If you're looking for longer cut running shorts, you can find them here, as well as race-ready or marathon shorts (lots of pockets) and other attire.

charity teams

Joints in Motion (www.arthritis.org): A 20 week training program to benefit The Arthritis Foundation. Train to walk or run a marathon or participate in a challenging hiking event.

MS Walk (www.nationalmssociety.org): The National Multiple Sclerosis Society's MS Walk is a great tool for recruiting a group of friends to join you in a fitness endeavor that also gives back to your community.

Team ACS (www.cancer.org/TeamACS): Team ACS is an online fundraising tool which allows people participating in a variety of events to raise funds to support the fight against cancer.

Team in Training (www.teamintraining.org): Enjoy a four or five month training program and free airfare and lodging to one of over 60 accredited events throughout the country. In exchange, you raise funds for leukemia, lymphoma and myeloma research.

Train to End Stroke (www.StrokeAssociation.com): A 20 week training program which benefits The Stroke Association. An expert coaching staff will train you for a full or half marathon.

general resources

Runner's World (www.runnersworld.com): This is one of the best overall running sites on the internet, so take some time to explore the different resources it has to offer.

Dress the Runner is a nifty tool for determining what to wear for your workout for specific weather conditions. With ShoeFinder, simply enter your gender, shoe size and training habits, and they aid you in finding the best shoe for your needs. This site also offers a listing of specialty running stores in each state.

gear & accessories

Heart rate monitors (www.everythingfitness.com): A large array of heart rate monitors ranging in cost from under $50 to over $200.

ID tags (www.RoadID.com): These guys mean business. They offer quite a variety of ID products, from wrist and ankle bands to ID tags for shoes, as well as other high visibility reflective gear. Take time to check out the testimonials, too. Worthy reading!

Shoes (www.MyRunningShoe.com): An online source for hard-to-find or recently discontinued running shoes.

marathon directories

Marathon listing (www.firsttimemarathoners.com): A fun site to visit. It provides a generous list of both U.S. marathons and international ones. It also has a pace chart to help you determine your approximate finishing time.

Race calendar (www.marathonguide.com): A useful calendar of marathons in each month. Check out the First Marathoners section if you need a dose of inspiration. You'll find lots of heartwarming accounts of first marathon experiences.

Walker-friendly marathons (www.marathonwalking.com/marathons.html and www.marathonguide.com/news/exclusives/WalkerFriendlyMarathons.cfm)

noteworthy events

Avon Walk for Breast Cancer (www.avonwalk.org): A two day event held in nearly 200 cities across the country. The goal is to walk at least the distance of a marathon (or more) in only two days...and it's for a good cause!

Komen Race for the Cure (www.komen.org): This is the largest series of 5K runs/ fitness walks in the country. Your participation helps raise funds and awareness for the fight against breast cancer. Survivors are also honored at these events. Plus they give out the most beautiful pink and green bandanas (a new design each year)...a lovely reminder of such a noble cause.

Breast Cancer 3 Day (www.the3day.org): The Susan G. Komen Breast Cancer Foundation also sponsors a 3-day walk covering a total of 60 miles. The people we know who have participated in this walk will tell you it is a life-changing experience.

More Marathon (www.nyrr.org/race/2005/moremarathon/index.php): Hosted by More Magazine and the New York Road Runners Club, this is the first and only race of its kind—for women over forty. Participate in the full or half marathon or the healthwalk. Held in New York in the spring.

Nike Women's Marathon (www.nikemarathon.com): From an on-course chocolate mile and Pedi-Care station to the Finisher Necklace by Tiffany & Co., what better way to spend an October weekend in San Francisco? Join over 9,000 other women to run a full or half marathon to benefit the Leukemia & Lymphoma Society.

running clubs

Cool Running (www.coolrunning.com): A cool site, if you ask us. You'll find running clubs in every state. There's even a free online running journal to keep tabs on your progress. Additionally, you can take advantage of their online coaching, a convenient option if you live in a remote area.

Pace teams (www.clifbar.com/paceteams): This is a great spot to learn more how pace teams work. However, you do not necessarily have to register ahead to run with a pace team; ask at the expo if pace teams will participate and just look for them on race morning.

Road Runners Club of America (www.rrca.org): Road Runners Club of America boasts over 670 running clubs and 160,000 members. A huge database of clubs in every state, including Alaska, Hawaii, Puerto Rico and Guam.

Walking (www.walking.about.com/cs/clubs/a/companions.htm): Having trouble finding a walking companion? About Walking can hook you up with online walking companions. It also offers loads of other resources.

training strategies

Galloway method (www.jeffgalloway.com): Jeff Galloway's official site. This will explain in detail his popular run/walk strategy.

Marathon walking (www.marathonwalking.com): This site provides a variety of training plans and tips for those interested in walking their first marathon. There's also information on racewalking. Be sure to click on The Walking Site to check out the

12 week Beginner's Challenge if you need some extra motivation.

Strength training (http://compuserve.lhj.com/lhj/health/): Click on Health & Fitness Slide Show, then again on Total Body Workout. A beginner's strength training program for women that is clearly demonstrated.

what to do with your medal?

Fond Memories Graphics (www.fondmemoriesgraphics.com): This company offers shadow boxes and bib frames in which to display your marathon memories.

Crossing the Line (www.CTLproducts.com): These personalized event products are an awesome way to remember your accomplishments. You provide the photo and medal and they do the rest. Beautiful designs.

acknowledgments

We would like to thank the coaching expertise and endless wisdom of Karen Cosgrove. She never doubted our ability to complete our first marathon and convinced us of that weekly--through tears, falls, sprains and scratches. It is truly not enough for her to celebrate in her own incredible accomplishments; but she shepherds others to the finish lines of their own dreams.

We would also like to thank the many people who provided us with invaluable help: Dr. Liz Applegate, Director of Sports Nutrition, University of California, Davis and Runner's World contributor; walking coach Beth Eidmiller; and Daniel R. Brauning, MPT, ATC, of Oxford Physical Therapy. We especially thank Julie Isphording for her insight and witticisms. Her talent extends well beyond the running trails.

We feel privileged to have trained with the Leukemia and Lymphoma Society's Team in Training of Cincinnati. Thank you for opening our worlds just a bit wider. And we thank all those tender souls at arm's length, teaching by example the grace with which we yearn to walk.

How do we even begin to pay tribute to all the women who so graciously shared their own marathon memories with us? Here's to Dee, Jerri, Jeannie and all the Women in Motion. And here's to Sabrina, who taught us in death what many fail to learn in life. Barbara , Paula, Fran, and Gerry Ann…thank you! And Bettie…never stop dancing! Thank you Wendy and Karen for gifting us with your wonderful story. And here's to Carrie and her amazing mother Katie, who taught us all to look for magic.

And thank you Kate Palandech, for believing in us!

Alyce would like to thank:

- the Olive Tree gang, who never doubted the athlete in me despite years of evidence to the contrary;
- the many friends who showed their support with simple cards, emails, survival packages, phone calls, finish line appearances and most importantly, contributions to the Leukemia and Lymphoma Society;
- the girls from Georgia Tech, Xavier and Notre Dame whose enthusiasm kept me running;
- my coworkers who patiently listened to my aches and pains and shared in the excitement of my journey;
- Sarah, who took us under her wing for six months and waited to hold my hand as we crossed the finish line;
- Jenny, Jen and Erin for making us feel 20 again;

- Barry and Kris, who reveled in our success and celebrated our victory as though it were their own;
- Marc for his belief in me from the start, his high fives at the end and his friendship in between;
- Curtis for showing us the sheer joy of running with friends, both old and new;
- Wendy for her humor, her heart, her devotion and her friendship…and for always letting me be the fastest;
- Dad, who was at my side every step of the way and cheered as I crossed the finish line from the best seat in the house;
- God, for keeping us healthy, for answering our prayers, and for opening our eyes along the way.

Wendy would like to thank:
- All my friends and family who contributed to my marathon fundraising, listened to my training woes, and at the end of the day filled my ziplock bags with ice and my glass with wine;
- My mother for instilling in me a passion for writing, Nathan Bowling for his computer savvy, Robin Acree for coming to the "pig rescue," June Williams for a priceless day of laughter and exhaustion (you can stop wearing your medal now), and Kathy Clements, who runs a race daily

much harder than any marathon and never gives up;

- Nathalie Robbins, someone I'll forever keep on my mentor committee

- Alyce, for laughing at my jokes but never at my dreams;

- I also thank my earthly father, the late Clifton Williams, for always believing in me… and my Heavenly Father, for proving that failure never results from believing in Him.

Index

A

B

C

E

F

G

H

I

J

K

L

R

S

T